Cindy Ross has her own unique way of capturing the spirit of backpacking. It's a ground-level view of life, the backpacker's view. Her words are comforting and homey, almost like you've heard them somewhere before. Think of her approach as "common-sense backpacking." For readers venturing into the outdoors for the first time, Cindy's words are full of acceptance, love, and security. She'll start you down the trail with a level head and a full heart. The rest is up to you.

—John Viehman, Executive Editor
Backpacker magazine

Ross writes with an ear for dialogue and an eye for detail, pulling the reader into the physical and emotional landscape of long-distance hiking.

—*Publishers Weekly* about Cindy Ross'
book *Journey on the Crest*

CYCLING
by Arlene Plevin
RUNNING
by John Schubert
SAILING
by Michael B. McPhee

Forthcoming

CLIMBING

CROSS-COUNTRY SKIING

SCUBA DIVING

SKIING

HIKING

A CELEBRATION OF THE SPORT AND THE WORLD'S BEST PLACES TO ENJOY IT

---

by CINDY ROSS

Illustrations by Frederick Carlson

Travel section by John Harlin

A RICHARD BALLANTINE/BYRON PREISS BOOK

To Colleen, without your companionship
I would have been lost.

Cindy Ross has written extensively about hiking the Appalachian Trail (*A Woman's Journey*) and the Pacific Crest Trail (*Journey on the Crest*). She has hiked more than 6,000 miles and is a contributing editor for *Backpacker*. She lives with her husband and two children near the Appalachian Trail in Pennsylvania.

Hiking: A Celebration of the Sport and the World's Best Places to Enjoy It

Series Editor: Richard Ballantine
Design Director: Byron Preiss
Editor: Babette Lefrak
Associate Editor: Brendan Healey
Contributor: Peter Oliver
Designers: Stephen Brenninkmeyer and Nancy Novick
Illustrator: Frederick Carlson
Cover Design: Fabrizio La Rocca
Cover Photograph: John Kelly/The Image Bank
Cover Illustrator: Marco Marinucci

Special thanks to Kristina Peterson, Publisher of Fodor's; Michael Spring, Editorial Director of Fodor's; Nin Chi, Kathy Huck, Nellie Kurtzman, Rosana Ragusa, Jessica Steinberg.

Portions of this book previously appeared in other forms in Backpacker, *and* Walking.

Special Sales
Fodor's Travel Publications are available at special discounts for bulk purchases (100 copies or more) for sales promotions or premiums. Special editions, including personalized covers, excerpts of existing guides, and corporate imprints, can be created in large quantities for special needs. For more information write to Special Marketing, Fodor's Travel Publications, 201 East 50th Street, New York, 10022. Inquiries from Canada should be sent to Random House of Canada, Ltd., Marketing Department, 1265 Aerowood Drive, Mississauga, Ontario L4W 1B9. Inquiries from the United Kingdom should be sent to Fodor's Travel Publications, 20 Vauxhall Bridge Road, London, England, SWIV 2SA.

MANUFACTURED IN THE UNITED STATES OF AMERICA.
10 9 8 7 6 5 4 3 2 1

CONTENTS

BEGINNINGS

THE HIKING LIFE

HIKING FOR TOMORROW

25 GREAT HIKES OF THE WORLD

HIKING

BEGINNINGS

It all began with the Appalachian Trail. . . . He wasn't an extremely tall man, but his backpack towered over his bearded face. He was in a hurry and it didn't appear he wanted to stop and chat. He only half turned to answer the questions my hiking friends asked, after he had already passed us on the trail. My friends were very interested in knowing how far he'd come.

"Georgia," was the man's quick answer.

"That's great, good luck to you," my friends yelled to him. With that, he turned and trotted off, socks dangling from the outside of his pack, fresh fruit swaying in plastic bags so it wouldn't get crushed inside.

This man was doing what I had heard could be done, but I never had seen any proof that someone actually did. Perhaps I, too, could hike 2,100 miles from Georgia to Maine. That day triggered something deep inside me. A seed was planted. From then on, it was always there. The trail. In the back of everything else that drifts and sifts through a young person's mind along with dreams of the future, this seed began to grow.

About that time, Colleen came into my life. It was a time when high school popularity meant almost everything. A girl had to be dating a football hero to be anyone, and it helped if she were a cheerleader. I wasn't an outcast, but I didn't tote pom-poms either. The cattiness of the girls my age left me feeling there had to be something more.

Colleen and I were too young to drive and barely old enough to date. What we could do was walk and that was a way to get some of the freedom our young spirits yearned for. We used to meet summer evenings on the mountainside halfway between our homes. We'd walk to the town reservoir, climb the chain link fence, and skinny-dip in the cool, black water. Afterward, we'd roll our sleeping bags out under the pines and sleep until the crows woke us. Then we'd be off on our bicycles to our summer jobs. The transition from life under the open sky to the routine of work was very abrupt and obvious. Even at that young age, the unspoken rules of society on how to dress and how to behave felt burdensome to us. We were delighted to discover that there was a different way to live, a different way to feel. Outdoors, we felt wild and free. Running back and forth in the grass on top of the dam wall, air-drying our wet, naked bodies; the smell of sun cooking pine needles; the low, morning rays of warm light: this was how we wanted to live—close to nature. The outdoors was a marvelous thing to discover so early in our lives.

Colleen and I went for walks in the woods to talk about what was happening to us, trying to understand our feelings and why we were so different from our peers. We felt oddly misplaced in time. We thought we'd make much better pioneer women than secretaries. On our hikes, we were becoming women. We were on a road to self-discovery, creating who we are today. Those walks and talks could have taken place on the concrete sidewalks of my suburban neighborhood, but because we hiked in the woods, hiking and the woods became sacred to me.

At the same time, I was also experiencing the normal friction with my parents. My father's principles and mine seemed opposite. He was concerned with the lint on my navy blue coat when we went to church, and I was upset that he judged my friends by their long hair. "Why would you want to look stupid?" he'd ask them directly when they came to visit, embarrassing me to death. I saw him as closed-minded; he sometimes saw me as irresponsible. What we did have in common was our love of the outdoors, and we were wise enough to nurture that similarity. When my father and I took our guns on walks in the woods during hunting season, we seemed to forget our differences in opinion.

We hiked slowly in the deep snow, rifles slung over our shoulders as the flakes came down softly and silently. We held hands and gazed at the white landscape as the horizon melted from land into sky. I didn't care if I shot a deer. In fact, I hoped I wouldn't have to. All I cared about was that my daddy and I smiled quietly to each other through the falling snow and his warm hand was wrapped around mine.

We never got along better than on those hikes. They were the glue that kept our father-daughter relationship strong through those rocky years. In retrospect, I think his seeming displeasure with some of the things I did as a youth was borne of his frustration and disappointment that he couldn't live the carefree life I was choosing.

In my sophomore year of high school I began to date a senior named Chris. Most of our days together revolved

around hikes. We had very little money and infrequent access to a car. But where we lived, there were many places to hike, and we walked for miles and miles in the evenings on horse trails, over golf courses, and around lakes. These hikes made me feel comfortable in the night, in the dark, and made the outdoors feel like home.

Chris and I went our separate ways but I continued to use hikes to screen men all the rest of my single years. In my twenties, I worked in a popular bar-restaurant for a while. Any man who came in with a beard and hiking boots, and who seemed halfway polite and interested, was worth a trial run. I could ask a man out on a hike, and he wouldn't feel threatened. It seemed like the perfect way to spend those initial hours with a stranger when I wasn't sure if I wanted to be alone with him in his apartment, or if he might be too shy to hold a continuous flow of conversation across a dinner table. Conversation flows more freely when people walk side by side, and eye contact isn't necessary to be polite. Walking stimulates thoughts and promotes openness—a good situation for sharing and discovering what another person is all about. It was a safe first date, a good test to see if I wanted to spend more time with someone. If he didn't like hiking, he wasn't for me—I needed him to share my love of nature and the outdoors. I wanted that kind of sensitivity in a man. It was a prerequisite for my long-term affection.

Without my being aware of it, hiking became an important vehicle toward understanding myself and others. My time spent walking in the woods with people led to richer relationships and a clearer vision of who I

The Appalachian Trail

Remote for detachment
Narrow for chosen company
Winding for leisure
Lonely for contemplation
The trail leads not merely north and south
But upward to the body, mind, and soul of man.
                                        —Harold Allen

The Appalachian Trail (AT) is the longest continually marked footpath in the world. It travels from Georgia to Maine through fourteen states for 2,100 miles and hugs the gentle ridges of the Appalachian Mountains, guiding you through long, winding forested tunnels. It has some of the richest vegetation in the world and some of the most varied. It is a highly accessible trail, for it is within reach of the majority of people residing in the urban areas of the eastern United States.

There is a sense of security on the trail. Even in storms that rake the treetops, the forest canopy protects you from winds that could blow you around in more open, exposed country. There is a feeling of protection as tree branches intertwine above your head and bring you shade and escape from the heat.

The mountains of the AT are quite low in many places, especially in the middle states, and most of the land is gentle and rolling. Still, the trail itself is often difficult. The AT is an old trail, built before much was known about erosion control, and so it often follows the lay of the land: straight up and straight down mountains. It is essentially a mountain and peak trail.

It may rain more in the Appalachians than in other mountains of the country, but there are 225 three-sided log and stone shelters along the way that offer protection from the elements and enable you to stand upright (as opposed to lying in a tent) and socialize when the weather's inclement. Many towns and roads cross the trail, so you can depart for a good meal, clean clothes, a shower, and a bed.

The AT is a very social trail. Many folks begin in Georgia to hike the entire trail and follow in an undulating wave all the way to Maine for five to six months. You have a choice of camping and enjoying company, or camping on your own, in solitude. It is a good trail to learn on. A good trail to discover who you are and what hiking and backpacking are all about.

For more information about the Appalachian Trail contact: Appalachian Trail Conference, P.O. Box 403, Watertown, MA 02272, tel.: 617/926-8200.

was and what I wanted and needed out of life. Hiking was not only very important to me, it was necessary and irreplaceable.

Sometime during all the walking and reflecting, I decided that a long distance hike would be best shared with a new husband. What a great way to break in a marriage. We would learn about each other and get really close right from the start. That was my game plan. My honeymoon would be spent hiking the entire Appalachian Trail. Now all I had to do was wait for my Vibram-soled prince to come hiking into my life. People used to ask me, "What are you going to do if you fall in love with a man who doesn't hike?" My answer was simple. "I won't." I wasn't concerned in the least. I knew by that time that nature and the outdoors had to be a part of my life for me to be happy. I wanted my partner to share my major loves, and hiking was one of them.

Well, the years rolled by and no one was too quick to get me down the aisle. Meanwhile, the Appalachian Trail was pulling strongly on my heart. My younger brother said he'd go, so after we bought his gear we slept out one summer night to give it a try. He found his sleeping bag so constricting that he walked home in the middle of the night, announced he wasn't going on the trail with me, and sold his equipment shortly afterward. I was frustrated again.

At twenty-two, I was an art student at the Pennsylvania Academy of Fine Arts in Philadelphia. I didn't hate the time and the space that I was in; I loved learning to paint and I even came to love the people in the city. But after two years I began to realize that what was drastically missing from Philadelphia and my life were wild spaces. I could no longer live without them.

About that time, my childhood friend Colleen said she'd really like to go on the Appalachian Trail hike with me, and from that moment on we were dedicated and determined. Over the course of a year we gathered food for our trip and dried it in a dehydrator that I had built. Besides all sorts of fruits and vegetables, we dried home-made cookies, crackers, granola, fruit leathers, and jerky from a deer that I hunted—250 pounds of food in all.

I felt that I had enough experience. I had been back-packing for several years before our departure, but never for more than a three-day weekend. But I was certain of two things: I loved to walk, and I loved to be close to nature. Except for physical injury, I couldn't foresee any reason for not reaching our goal, and I felt that I couldn't be better prepared. We packed the food in boxes and instructed our folks to mail them general delivery to post offices in towns along the way just before we headed out on the trail. Every four to eight days we would drop off the trail to resupply. To get into shape, we did all of our errands by foot, instead of by car, and wore loaded packs and our hiking boots. We sure got the stares, but we didn't care. We were involved in our dream. Half the joy of our adventure came from preparing.

The trip started off fine. But after six hundred miles, Colleen left our partnership for personal reasons. I was alone again with a dream that was meant to be shared.

I was very sad, so sad that I tried to hike my sadness

Preparation

• *Before hitting the trail, put on your new hiking boots, weigh down your new pack, and go walk uneven terrain. This way you can adjust the pack straps and belts and find a comfortable fit. Most packs come in different sizes, and if you're a small person trying to lug a large-sized pack, it may not fit. Find out before hitting the trail. The same goes for boots. New ones usually require a break-in period before they are comfortable, and in some cases, boots that fit fine in the store turn brutal after three miles on the trail. To be safe, if you're heading out with new boots, wrap your heels with duct tape before a heel blister starts to show. And carry spare duct tape wrapped around a water bottle.*

• *Pack lighter, not heavier. Many inexperienced hikers try to carry much more weight than is comfortable or safe. The result can be a less than pleasant trip or a pulled muscle. A good rule of thumb is to carry roughly one-fifth to one-quarter of your body weight. You can increase the weight to as much as one-third of your weight as you get stronger.*

• *Look at each piece of gear and ask yourself if there's a lighter item that can replace it. Or can you make that particular piece of gear lighter? Ounces add up to pounds. Trim extra-wide borders off maps; cut the handle off your* toothbrush; trim unused pockets, cuffs, and belt loops off spare clothing; use a plastic spoon and cup instead of metal ones.

• Develop a system for packing, and know how to put your tent up in the dark. Fill your pack the same way each time you use it, and try to avoid stuffing things into pockets; this system will save you time when a storm hits and you're trying to find your rain gear. It's nice to know, too, just where that flashlight is hiding, because night can fall fast.

• Carry a hiking staff. On rocky terrain, it can serve as a third leg for better balance. When stepping over rocks or logs, you can poke around for snakes. You can use it to flick limbs and branches off the trail. It can form a third leg for stream crossings, and substitute as a pack rest for your backpack when no trees are around.

away. I was doing twenty-mile days, never stopping to rest longer than ten to fifteen minutes at a time. I'd kill myself to reach a shelter every night in the hope of camping with other people. I wanted to see others so badly that I imagined I heard voices ahead on the trail. "Hello! How ya doin'?" I yelled when I saw someone approaching, long before they were in earshot. I remembered a quote I read in a hiking guide, and the real meaning of Jim Podlesney's words hit home hard: "How can (you) describe the psychological factors a person must prepare for . . . the despair, the alienation, the anxiety and especially the pain, both physical and mental, which slices to the very heart of the hiker's volition, which are the real things that must be planned for? No words can transmit those factors, which are more a part of planning than the elemental rituals of food, money, and equipment. . . . "

I couldn't run away from feelings or fears, however. Because of pushing myself into big mileage days, I continually tripped from fatigue. Finally, I broke my foot. Now I would be forced to end my misery and go home. I didn't consciously think this at the time, of course, but I believe today that my injury was brought on by my subconscious need to end my suffering. I could now go home and get the love, affection, and support I needed from my family.

Contrary to the profile of most long distance hikers, I am not introverted by nature. I like conversation. I like company. I like to share. I was comfortable with myself, I just didn't enjoy being alone as much as I enjoyed companionship, especially when my aloneness wasn't by choice. I learned a very important lesson on that journey:

I need people. I can't make it in this world alone, and I don't want to try.

After my foot and my heart healed, I returned to Virginia where I had left off, and hiked to Pennsylvania—four hundred more miles—before the end of the season. I hiked solo then, too, but I met and walked with other hikers off and on. I had changed, and felt at peace with myself. I truly wanted to be there and didn't care if I was alone. That made all the difference.

The following year, 1979, I returned with JoAnn, another woman friend, to hike the remaining 1,000 miles. JoAnn had a hard time; her body wasn't used to such exercise. Her knees fell apart. She suffered a relapse of an earlier bout with tonsillitis. She was allergic to insect bites, which swelled up to the size of half dollars. Every time we stopped for a break, she fell fast asleep from exhaustion. Her determination amazed me. Quitting was not in her vocabulary, but it took her almost 500 miles of walking until she felt strong enough to really enjoy the hike.

My personality and presence were sometimes hard on JoAnn. She was used to more private space and found me a bit overwhelming at times. Hiking with a committed partner is not easy. People can't get away from each other for any length of time and the fatigue that accompanies such physical exertion makes it easy to be irritable. But I felt that little could be gained from separating. It's too easy to leave a hiking partner every time something goes sour. We would never have learned to communicate or coexist if we had split up. I looked at that hike as a training ground for future relationships.

As the miles rolled by, our commitment to finish the

14

The Perfect Partner

Start looking for a partner for a long hike as soon as possible. It will take time to talk to friends, search the local hiking clubs, or join organizations whose publications print want-ads for hiking partners. Get to know your potential partner well, preferably with practice hikes (especially the long weekend kind) that will determine if your individual hiking styles can be synchronized. The most successful hiking teams have usually spent many miles on the trail together before the long journey.

Keeping a partner can be more difficult than actually reaching your goal. There is so much compromising along the way, and the need for communication is so strong, that even married couples have been known to split up on long-distance hikes. Some people choose to go it alone, but having a partner is safer than traveling by yourself. And it's fun to share the experience with a friend. Just realize that at any point your partner could quit and you will be faced with a long solo journey.

hike grew stronger and so did our friendship. When all was said and done, there was no greater pleasure for me than having JoAnn by my side.

JoAnn showed me that the real beauty of hiking the Appalachian Trail was not just living in harmony with nature, but with each other. Our success couldn't be measured by merely reaching Mount Katahdin in Maine, but rather by fulfilling this mutual dream together.

On a warm, sunny Labor Day, that dream finally came true. No air moved on the monolith of Mount Katahdin. The granite radiated heat back to me as I grabbed the iron handholds planted in the boulders. I pulled my body across the rock and through the Gateway. From there on out, we were above the timberline. My muscles had been pushed beyond their limits, and my legs shook from the anxiety and excitement.

Small tufts of alpine flowers nestled between the rocks at our feet as we followed the mile-long, open peneplain to the summit. I stared down at them, and my eyes welled with tears. JoAnn came up from behind and asked, "How are you doin', Cindy?"

"Tired. Real tired."

"Me, too."

We had slept little the night before, awake with anticipation. The 5,200-foot climb and the impact of the day were wearing us out. As the drama mounted, we walked more closely together. At the summit we collapsed, embracing the sign and each other.

"HURRAY! IT IS FINIS!"

I was never the same again.

When I stood on top of that mountain and ran my

The Pacific Crest Trail

The Pacific Crest Trail (PCT) is a 2,600-mile trek from Mexico to Canada. It is far from its eastern relative, the Appalachian Trail, in more than just miles. Instead of 1,000 long-distance hikers leaving its southern terminus annually, there are perhaps twenty. There are no blazes to speak of, few signs, and only four shelters.

Nearly everything about the PCT breathes wilderness: long stretches of roadless areas, seas of jagged granite peaks, glaciers, herds of elk, desert crossings, meadows of wildflowers. It begins by snaking through the high desert of the Traverse Ranges. One day you'll be up at 9,000 feet, in snow, and the next day you'll be down in the desert in the scorching heat. After about 400 miles of these radical changes, it drops into the left arm of the Mojave Desert, where temperatures can reach 115° to 120° by noon in the late spring.

Yet the treadway is considerably easier than that of any trail built in the East, for it's graded to at least 10 percent to accommodate stock animals. The skill of using map and compass is advisable, however, for unlike hiking on the AT, where 2" x 6" white painted blazes guide you all the way, the PCT can be difficult to locate. In the south, cow paths are more heavily traveled than the treadway, and can easily throw a hiker off course. Leaving the desert, you climb into the Sierra Nevada Mountains, which boast the highest peak in the lower forty-eight, Mount Whitney (14,494 feet). Here, the trail can be buried under snow until August, forcing the hiker to cross very steep grades and climb near-vertical mountain sides with the gradual, graded trail far below.

Leaving the 800-mile-long Sierra, the trail then takes you into the mysterious and grand land of the volcanic Cascades. Once you're into the North Cascades of Washington, the mountains are lower (7,000 feet) than the Sierra, but are very serrated and potentially treacherous. The trail is dynamited high, near the ridgelines and takes only a little bit of newly fallen autumn snow to send a hiker and an avalanche roaring down the sides.

The PCT forces maturity upon the hiker. The AT is a more challenging and demanding thru-hike, but there is a thrill and a magnificent beauty to the unrivaled wildness of the PCT.

finger across the routed wooden sign that pointed south and read, Springer Mountain, Georgia, 2,100 miles, I knew what had happened. I realized suddenly that I could have a dream and if I worked hard enough and believed in it deeply enough, it would come true. All it took was a strong passion and a lot of perseverance. Hiking gave me many gifts, but the most priceless one was this incredible self-confidence and belief in myself. I wondered where my limits were and if I even had any.

After I returned from the Appalachian Trail, I began to paint scenes from my journey and to have solo art shows. I wrote and illustrated my first book, *A Woman's Journey,* taken from my trail journals, and began lecturing and giving slide presentations around the country. It thrilled me to see that I could derive an income from my beloved sport.

Then the Pacific Crest Trail began pulling at my heart. That trail stretches from Mexico to Canada for 2,600 miles through California, Oregon, and Washington. It traverses the Mojave Desert, the backbone of the Sierra Nevada Range, and the volcanic wonderland of the Cascades. I planned to hike it in two halves, which would allow me to stretch the trip out and give me time to write and take photographs for a new book on the Pacific Crest Trail. After I completed my first stretch of 1,200 miles in 1982 and returned home, something occurred that I had been dreaming about ever since those early walks with Colleen. That size-twelve hiking boot walked into my life to stay.

Todd and I had first met two years before. When I returned from the Appalachian Trail, I had moved to a farmhouse by the trail in Pennsylvania, where I could write and paint. Occasionally I'd cruise through town where the trail crossed and stop to see if any hikers were passing through. When I felt like company, I'd bring them home and share a home-cooked dinner with them. When I brought home Todd, he had just turned nineteen and was shy and boyish. He hardly spoke all evening.

Two years later, we both happened to be on the Pacific Crest Trail at the same time, although our paths never crossed. Because of a broken foot, his journey was cut short and he returned home to a hiking conference where we met again. Every hiker there was wrapped up in the Appalachian Trail, but the two of us couldn't keep our minds off the trail out west. Since we lived fairly close to each other, we decided that when his foot got better a hike would be in order, where we could talk and reminisce some more.

After our hike, I said to my mother, "That's the kind of guy I ought to marry. He loves the mountains, he loves to hike, and he's kind and sweet."

"Well, what's wrong with him?" she asked.

"He's young and he doesn't talk much."

"He'll get older," she said, "and he'll learn to talk."

Our honeymoon was spent (as I had dreamed) on a hike traversing 1,400 miles through the Cascade Mountains. Living together twenty-four hours a day for four months was a very intense initiation. We couldn't escape to a car or a job when we argued. We were forced to work things out. We couldn't run to friends or mothers. We had only each other. On the trail, we experienced everything together. We watched the same breathtaking sunsets and we battled through the same lightning storms. We crawled into our sleeping bags feeling the same exhaustion, and we felt the same joy at diving into a refreshing mountain lake. It bonded us—those four months of hiking. It made us want nothing to ever come between us and it made us believe there was little we could dream about that couldn't come true.

In the years that followed, many of the major events in my life were connected to hiking. No wonder that in time it became such a deeply integrated part of my life and my soul. It turned into far more than a recreational sport for me. It was a rite of passage.

Todd and I conceived our first baby, Sierra, on a hike. We went to the Outer Banks of North Carolina and backpacked down the skinny barrier islands of Cape Hatteras with the sole intent of starting a family!

There were miles of deserted beaches to hike, with easy walking on the hard sand down by the crashing waves at low tide. There were large whelk shells to collect, sand sculptures to build, and lots of love to make in the dunes. Sierra was conceived among all that beauty.

All through my pregnancy, I walked. While my daughter was growing inside of me, I took her for daily hikes in the forest where we lived along the Appalachian Trail, and I told her of the dancing light and the wind in the trees and the buttercups she would someday see for herself.

We wanted Sierra to be born at a birth center with a midwife in attendance. I was told that if she were more

Hiking Trail

• *Limber up. At the start of each hike, stretch your hamstrings, calves, feet, shoulders, and back muscles.*

• *Set the pace by your slowest member. To keep a group together, you may have to shift some heavy gear from a hiker who's lagging behind to one who's continually shooting far ahead. Cooperation is important.*

• *A normal backpacking pace is one and one-half to two miles per hour, but it's quite common to slow down to one mile an hour on hills. A pace as fast as three miles an hour is possible on level ground or slight inclines.*

• *Be reasonable. When setting a goal for your hike, give some thought to the possibility that you may not reach your goal; it may be beyond your capabilities, or the capabilities of someone in your group. An injury or illness could occur, or, more likely, the weather could take a turn for the worse. Plan a bail-out route or a shorter schedule, just in case.*

• *If a group of you are hiking, eliminate backtracking by splitting into two parties. One group is dropped off at one point and the car is parked at the opposite point. The key is exchanged when groups pass on the trail. Or use two cars, parking one at Point A and the other at Point B, then switch keys in the middle.*

than two weeks overdue, I'd have to go into a hospital and get labor induced. But I didn't want to do this, so when the two weeks passed I drank a bottle of castor oil and took thirty-two herbal tablets to kick my body into gear and convince Sierra to come out. I went on a hike, one that I'd never want to repeat, but the oil and tablets worked. Sierra was born the next day.

Before she was conceived, it used to frighten me to think about being a parent and possibly having to give up my beloved sport for many years. I feared I'd grow fat and lazy from inactivity. Every mother I knew told me I'd be unable to do many of the things I had done when I was childless. But there were some things, like hiking, that I was determined not to part with. I would adapt and conform, but I would not abandon it.

When Sierra was four months old, we took her on her first extended hike—sixty miles. Todd carried a seventy-pound pack full of heavy, soiled diapers. Our nights were often sleepless, since the gentle rocking of our walking made Sierra sleep too much during the daylight hours. There were no aids, like high chairs for feeding, and rocking chairs for consoling crying babies. But on our hikes we watched our baby's senses open wide to all the beauty nature offered. We saw her mesmerized by the sparkling sunlight on a lake. We watched her listen to singing brooks and follow the wind as it raked through the trees and fluttered the leaves. We listened to her caw to ravens and delight when they answered her back. We enjoyed watching her discover the textures of pine cones, big oak leaves, and sand in her toes.

When she turned one year old and learned to walk,

Biking with a Baby

The time had come for a new sport. On our last backpacking trip, my husband Todd lugged seventy pounds, while I toted forty-five, including our one-year-old daughter, Sierra. Todd was beginning to feel like a mule, or at least wish that he had one. We began wondering, Is it worth it?

What we needed was another way, other than our backs, to carry the diapers, clothes, extra bedding, and so on, and still enjoy some outdoor recreation. Plus, I was pregnant with Number Two and couldn't cinch a waist belt tight.

Bike touring—pulling Sierra behind us in a trailer—sounded like the sport we'd been looking for. We chose a Bike-Caboose trailer made in Idaho that could haul up to 150 pounds and had room for three kids (in case we had twins!).

We practiced on a mountaintop fire road nearby and quickly discovered that all hills had to be avoided for the sport to resemble anything close to fun. So, for our first adventure we chose the C & O Canal—a 185-mile dirt and gravel towpath that follows the Potomac River from Cumberland, Maryland, down into Washington, D.C. With campsites and water every five miles, and traveling level and downhill, our initiation into the sport couldn't have been any easier.

she had her own ideas of where to go and what to look at. "Hand!" she used to demand as she looked up at me, her big brown eyes shining. She'd negotiate the deck stairs on her fanny and pull her mother down the path. At a patch of mint, she'd break off a furry leaf and suck it against her nostrils. "Mmmm!" Pine cones, sticks, and fallen leaves would grab her attention, and she squatted down to examine each one she came across. Still pulling her mother along, she'd trot down the path, diapered bottom sashaying, and stop to pick up a gypsy moth caterpillar to give it a kiss. A breeze would go by, rustling the aspen trees. "Wind!" she'd exclaim, and lift her head to the sky.

Sierra blessed our lives, and enhanced our love of hiking. It brought Todd and me great joy to share the things that we love most—flowers, wind, waterfalls, forests, and more—with our daughter. Seeing them through the eyes of a child who found wonder in the smallest bug made us appreciate nature as never before.

Over the years, hiking has become more than a sport to me. It has touched and influenced every part of my life, changing it and making it better. It gave me a husband, a child, and a way of living the free life I've grown to love on the trail.

It's difficult to return to a regimented life-style after your first long hike. The self-reliance we learned on the trail and our newfound thirst for freedom encouraged us to devise a more creative way of earning a living, so we could continue with this exciting process of truly living our lives.

We chose a simple life, growing much of our food on our land and building a log house ourselves. Free from

debt, we could spend our time as we wished. It was no longer necessary for us to work for someone else or to report to a job five days a week. Things had gone full circle, and like the long-distance Appalachian Trail hiker who changed my life when I was fifteen years old, we are now both inspiring others to get out on the trails and walk and discover the joys that we have found. Besides the magazine articles that Todd and I work on together, we teach backpacking at a local college, lecture and give slide presentations, and engage in a half dozen other creative activities to make a living.

All this occurred, I'm sure, because of the tremendous trait of self-reliance that hiking has instilled in us. We may never be rich, but that's not our goal. To be happy and free and love what we're doing with our lives is of paramount importance to us, and these have all been gifts from the trail.

TRAIL WISDOM

Babies

• Babies can ride on your back in a packlike carrier when they have no trouble holding and keeping their heads up, which is usually at four to six months of age. This is the easiest time to head for the trail, because a baby at this age isn't crawling and can be plopped on a foam pad to watch Mom and Dad set up camp. Once the baby starts crawling, one of the parents must be on constant watch.

• Don't even consider taking a baby backpacking unless you are a competent, experienced backpacker who has been in and successfully out of a few difficult situations. Your decision-making must be extra safe, extra cautious, and extra responsible when you take a baby or small child into the wilderness.

• The adult who's not carrying the baby must haul most of the gear: sleeping gear for three, clothes for three, food for three—get the idea? That pack will be extremely heavy. Single-parent backpacking is so difficult it's usually not worth the effort. Get an adult friend to go along and help share the burden.

• To get your children used to riding in the carrier, pack him around the house with you as you do your chores.

• Lift babies out of the pack every hour or two or every two to three miles. They'll be ready for a diaper change, a drink, something to eat, or a stretch. Going back into the pack after a break is often an occasion for fussing, no matter how much the child enjoys the ride. Sing a favorite song or shake a rattle and make a face while you adjust the harness. Once you are moving again, children will forget their displeasure.

• Plan to stop early in the day—no later than 5 P.M. There is a definite limit to the length of time a baby will be happy in a pack. After that limit, the child's mood will deteriorate rapidly.

• The gentle rocking motion of walking can lull your baby to sleep on the trail, but it can also result in too much sleep, making for a restless night. There is little you can do about this, except to go to sleep soon after your baby to ensure you get some rest.

• Babies sit relatively motionless when riding in a carrier, so check their bodies often. Feel the back of their necks or chests for excessive heat. Check their fingers, noses, and limbs to see if they are cold. Adjust clothing accordingly.

• The best trail clothing for an infant is one-piece, polyester pajamas with feet. Bring two sizes:

one close-fitting pair to act as long underwear and a thicker blanket sleeper for an outer layer. A cotton turtleneck under the sleeper is good for trapping heat and keeping the baby's neck warm.

• When toting your babies in child carriers, keep them warm by slipping adult-size wool socks over their legs—shoes and all. To keep the socks up, pin them to their pants. Attach a folding umbrella to the child carrier to protect your baby from rain and sun.

• When the weather is cool, keep a hat on your baby at all times. A balaclava offers the most warmth. In the summer, a hat with a wide brim will gives protection from the sun.

• For the hottest days of summer, a diaper and a shortsleeved, cotton T-shirt may be all that's necessary. Don't forget the sunscreen.

• Urine-soaked cloth diapers can be air-dried every night to cut down on pack weight, and a diaper can always be drying on the outside of your pack while you hike. Fasten with alligator clips purchased at the hardware store. Use single-layer diapers that open all the way up. Diaper covers or vinyl pants are a necessity with cloth diapers.

• Carry diapers with solid waste in bags to cut down on odor. Deal with them at home. Washing diapers in a stream is unthinkable, and carrying a large container to wash them in away from the water is impractical. If disposables are used, they must be packed out!

• For longer trips, choose a trail with a road intersection so a supply drop can be arranged. You can do this by hiding five-gallon buckets with tight, snap-on lids in the woods. Fill the buckets with food, clean diapers, and extra baby clothes for emergencies. Soiled diapers and trash can be left in the buckets and picked up after your hike is over.

• Always carry a fever reducer and a baby thermometer in your first aid kit.

• Camp far away from others so the inevitable middle-of-the-night crying fits won't disturb weary, sleeping hikers.

Toddlers

• Start with a day hike before attempting an overnighter. You'll learn what types of terrain your children can handle, how they respond to changes in the weather, and how much gear you'll need to carry. And those little items that make a trip better will pop into your head.

• Before your first trip, set up your tent in the yard and spend the night in it. Or let your children take naps in it so they aren't afraid to sleep in this strange, new place.

• When planning a trip with a toddler, expect to travel about one half mile per hour. Keep total trip mileage low. You might plan to hike only a mile, then set up camp. The more miles you attempt, the greater the chances you'll be toting a pack and your child. But do expect to carry your child part of the way out, because children always seem to run out of energy on the last leg of any trip.

• Like adults, children get a boost by eating snacks throughout the day. Slices of orange or a handful of raisins and peanuts will lift children's morale and keep them moving. Children cover a lot more ground than adults, since they usually run around a lot, so pump plenty of water and juice into your child to prevent dehydration.

• In the summer, dress your child in 100 percent cotton. Polyester and cotton blends are hotter, less absorbent, and less comfortable. Dress children in bright colors instead of earth tones so they're easy to spot if they wander off.

• Consider bringing along a friend for your child.

• Chemicals in insect repellents can be toxic to children. Visit a health food store and purchase a repellent made from natural ingredients.

• A child may need help stepping over rocks or maintaining balance on uneven surfaces. If two adults hold each end of a walking stick so it's horizontal to the ground, the child can walk between the adults, using the stick like a banister or handrail. □

Hiking Equipment Checklists

Day Hike:

Comfortable, loose-fitting clothes
Good walking shoes
Day pack/rucksack
One-liter water bottle
Rain gear
Food for the day
Lighter or waterproof matches
Small first aid kit, including moleskin
Toilet paper, backpacker's trowel

Additional Items:

Camera and film
Binoculars
Warm shirt
Hat
Bandanna
Map/guidebook

Overnight Hike:
Hiking boots
Backpack
Sleeping bag
Sleeping pad
Tent/tarp and groundcloth
Stove and fuel/fuel bottle
Cooking pot, pot gripper, scrubbie
Eating utensils/pocket knife
Water filter/purification tablets
More than adequate food for length
of the trip
Two one-liter water bottles
Cup
Raingear and pack cover
Change of clothing
Pair of loose-fitting long pants
Long-sleeved wool shirt/sweater
or pile jacket
Wool hat
Spare set of socks, including liners
Wool or poly/wool outer socks
One or two bandannas
Change of underwear
Long underwear, if season calls for it
Toilet paper, backpacker's trowel
Toothbrush and toothpaste
Nylon cord

Maps/guidebook
Flashlight with new batteries, spare
batteries, and bulb
Lighter/waterproof matches
Watch
First aid kit, including moleskin
Empty bread bag for trash

Optional:
In-camp shoes
Repair equipment kit
Sunscreen, skin lotion
Insect repellent
Camera and film
Journal and pen
Water bag
Sunglasses ☐

THE HIKING LIFE

When I hiked on the Appalachian Trail in 1979, my seventy-five-year-old grandmother used to light candles for me in church. She was sending up prayers for me to be safe, I'm sure, but mostly she prayed that I'd come home, not at the end of the trail, but right then. When I finally did, she and the rest of the family thought my long journeys would be over. Many people dream of hiking the entire AT their whole lives, and when they finally make the time, they're satisfied when they complete it and look for no more challenges. It's then time to get on with their lives, the lives they left behind.

After I met my husband Todd, my grandmother foolishly thought I would settle down. I was finally married—why should I need to go away? If she had stopped to think, she would have realized that Todd was as deeply in love with hiking as he was with me. If anything, the union made us wonderfully crazy, dreaming and planning about other hikes we wanted to take. Grandmom lit more candles when we talked about the Pacific Crest Trail, all in vain. When we built our house, she again hoped my hiking days were over. Poor Grandmom!

When we had a baby, surely we would forget these hiking adventures—surely no one would dream of taking a baby into the wilderness. Wrong again. We took Sierra hiking in the canyons of the desert Southwest when she was only eight months old.

I think by now, at eighty-seven, my grandmother is finally lighting candles and praying for other things more in need of divine aid. My family mostly leaves us alone now. Sometimes, they don't even realize we've been gone. Hiking has become a way of life for us, and they've grown used to that. Still, after all these years and all these thousands of miles, I think they continue to scratch their heads and wonder why. Why do we keep going back?

Except for a tiny crack to let in some air, the windows were rolled up tight. Still, our breath fogged the glass and obscured our view of the pelting rain. Thunder rumbled and lightning crackled around the car. Our baby in the back seat looked on and listened in amazement. Our backcountry permit lay on the dashboard, stating that we could spend one night on the rim above the Colorado River.

Half an hour later, the deluge had ended, and we climbed out of the car to load our packs. In the open, we could easily see which way the storm was moving— out over the canyon, in the direction we were heading.

Our two-mile trail across the meadow was flooded. A trickle turned into a swift stream. We walked above its banks, weaving in and out of clumps of arid-looking grass. Overhead, the clouds were breaking and we could see patches of blue and bright sunlight. Arches of color sprang out of the canyon on our left, and went back in on our right. The closer we got to the rim, the more distant and brilliant the rainbows became. We hurried our pace.

Just as we reached the slickrock, we hopped over the

Crossing Streams

Study a stream before starting across it—where the trail stops may not be the best route. Water usually moves most swiftly at the narrowest point of the stream. Where the stream widens the curent often slows and may be easier to walk through. Always loosen your shoulder straps and hip belt before fording, so you can throw off your pack if you get into trouble. Use your hiking staff or a stout stick as another leg; it will give you better balance when crossing swift water or when slippery rocks are underfoot.

To reduce the dragging effect of swift currents, take off excess clothing if the weather is warm. In cold weather, close-fitting long underwear will help keep you warm. To prevent slipping and to protect your feet, wear your boots, or switch to tennis shoes if they have good tread. Before venturing into the water remove your socks, then put them back on after you cross. Take each step slowly and deliberately. Your forward foot should be firmly planted before moving your rear foot. Never hurry.

rise and saw two bighorn sheep with full curls standing twenty feet away. The depressions in the slickrock held the rainwater and made the pool from which they drank a dreamy pink color, reflecting the evening sky. We stopped silently and gasped. Within seconds they moved away, hoofs clicking on the hard sandstone. We had no chance to catch our breaths, however, for as we lowered our eyes into the canyon we saw the most stupendous light show going on. Navy blue and purple storm clouds rolled above the deep canyon. Some walls were under their dark shadow, others glowed flame orange when long arms of sunlight broke through the clouds and touched them.

We watched for a long time. The storm rolled out and the rosy canyon grew dusty before we realized it was getting late and we needed to set up camp.

In the middle of the night I woke up and padded barefoot over to the rim. Huge, lurking walls rose in darkness while others were bathed in silvery moonlight. A mild breeze was blowing past me, over the edge, and down 2,200 feet to the river below.

At first light, I pulled my sleeping bag and pad out from their place between my daughter and my husband, and went over to the rim to watch the sunrise. The walls became more and more distinct as the sky grew brighter. I called to Todd and he carried Sierra and their bags out to the smooth rocks. We huddled in the cool morning air, watching the sun rise over the Colorado canyon. The two bighorn sheep suddenly topped a nearby rise and witnessed the beginning of a new day with us. We smiled at each other, feeling

very blessed for all that we had seen in just the last twelve hours.

I don't have such five-star experiences every time I take a hike. A hiker has to be out there a lot to see big wonders. Yet there are small wonders happening all around, all day long: cool breezes on a mountaintop drying the sweat on my damp back and perspired brow; gushing, cold spring water, refreshing me on a hot day; a crystal clear mountain lake that is so clean I can open my mouth wide and drink like a fish as I swim; the fog rolling down a mountain and settling into the valley below; the sound of spring peepers when the sun sinks low; and the call of whippoorwills in the middle of the night. The moments of magic, the patches of beauty, are endless. And the more I hike, the more my eyes and ears and all my senses open wide and become more sensitive to the beauty.

I like to think that whatever I experience in life contributes to the person I am, and the person I will someday be. My mind is like a sensitive emulsion sheet; whatever is exposed on it remains a part of me. How can I not be changed by so much beauty?

———————————

While driving home from Utah in 1990 from a backpacking trip, our car started to belch out white smoke just as we were topping Loveland Pass over the Rocky Mountains. By the time we reached home, dealers along the way had found $1,000 worth of repairs. Todd looked at me and said, "Damn cars, you never have this trouble when you're backpacking."

Safety on Long Hikes

• *Pack a good first aid book and kit. Before your trip, become familiar with the recommended treatments for common hiking injuries.*

• *Prepare for the worst. Always carry enough clothing for the worst possible weather during the time of year you're hiking. Don't rely on optimistic weather reports.*

• *Wear a watch because if the sky becomes overcast and the sun is obscured, darkness may catch you still on the trail. You don't want to be searching for your camp in the dark.*

• *Carry a whistle so you can signal for help if there's an emergency.*

• *Don't overextend yourself. Fatigue is like a tranquilizing drug; it impairs your judgment, and your reaction times are slower. Never hike more than eight hours a day. Also, many people push too hard when they first hit the trail because they're excited and charged up, but that initial exertion leaves them dragging for the rest of the multiday trip. Hike no more than five or six hours the first and second days of your trip.*

One of the most overwhelming feelings we have when we hike is a very strong sense of freedom. Something happens to me the moment I put on that pack. It doesn't even matter if it's heavy. As I adjust my shoulder straps and tighten my hip belt, I know that everything I need to survive is on my back: food, water, shelter, and clothing. It's a liberating experience—I can go anywhere. There are no mechanical parts to malfunction, no parts to replace, no service department to rip me off when they see my out-of-state plates. I am dependent on my legs and on my own good sense.

I am also free to spend my days as I wish, hiking long-and-hard miles or sunning by a lake. I can stop early to camp or hike late into the evening. I can eat when I'm hungry and rest when I'm tired. I can rise before dawn or sleep until noon. There are no alarm clocks or buzzers ringing, no schedules (except those I set myself), no telephones, meetings, or calendars full of commitments. My thoughts are my own as I hike. I can belt out a song and make believe I'm Joni Mitchell, or cry because I'm so happy to be where I am.

Along with the freedom of this life-style comes the necessity to adapt to sometimes less than ideal living situations. But what might appear unattractive in everyday life can seem downright comfortable and even luxurious on the trail.

When Todd was in Southern California on the Pacific Crest Trail, he and his hiking comrades got hit by a severe ice storm. They were heading into some high mountains, and, under these conditions, navigation would be extremely difficult. The freezing rain would soak their clothing,

and the fatigue of snow travel would drain their stamina, setting them up for possible hypothermia and exhaustion.

The only shelter for miles around was a forest service lavatory where the trail crossed the road, and it was heated. The far end of the room, by the electric wall heater, became their home for the next couple of days. They spread out their gear, rolled out their pads, shook out their bags, and fired up their stoves for supper. All the doors had been removed from the bathroom stalls. When travelers stopped in to relieve themselves, they checked the first few stalls. No doors. They kept moving toward the back of the room and toward Todd and his friends, looking for a private john. Most felt self-conscious, and returned to the stalls near the door. A few walked out. One man settled himself onto the toilet seat right next to Todd. While the man emptied his bowels, and while the hikers stirred their macaroni, he proceeded to tell them that all they needed to survive on the trail were dried apricots and a sack of potatoes. These would meet all their nutritive needs. The guys sat there, politely marveling at the simplicity of the idea, and tried to hold in their laughter over the oddness of the scene.

The storm finally cleared on the third day. When Todd and his friends went out to climb the mountain, all the trees were covered with ice, and shone like diamonds in the sun. It was a wonderland, the trail was easy to .negotiate, and the hikers were happy they had decided to wait it out, despite their less-than-ideal accommodations.

Life on the trail helps me to prioritize. I ask myself, what is most important; what do I need, not just what would I like. My personal safety comes first. Comfort falls

Hypothermia

Hypothermia is the leading cause of death in the outdoors. It occurs when the body's core temperature drops below 95° F. At this point, the body can't generate warmth, so its temperature continues to fall. Unless the victim is quickly warmed, he'll eventually die from exposure. To lessen the chances of hypothermia, eat before you get hungry, rest before you get tired, and if you feel a slight chill, put on more clothes—don't wait until you're cold and shivering.

One early sign of hypothermia is confused thinking. Many victims aren't aware of their condition and will say they feel fine. Watch companions for incoherent, slurred speech, violent fits of shivering, drowsiness, and exhaustion. If someone shows signs of hypothermia, stop hiking, get out of the wind and rain, and conserve the victim's energy. Give him hot drinks, but no alcohol (it's a depressant and he should be kept awake), and no coffee or tea (diuretics, which cause loss of body fluids). Get him into warm, dry clothing. Build a fire, or fill water bottles or canteens with hot water and place them against the chilled person. Give him high-energy foods to quickly resupply bodily fuel. If necessary, the victim and someone else should remove heavy clothing and crawl into a dry sleeping bag together; one person's body warmth can save another person's life.

somewhat lower on the list. Perhaps that's because what it takes to make me comfortable on the trail is far less than what it takes in normal life. I don't notice minor discomfort because I'm getting so many other gifts.

One of the most important freedoms I have is the ability to make my own decisions about my well-being and safety. I am totally responsible for myself. These critical decisions can be as seemingly insignificant as deciding when to put on rain gear or as important as how far to push myself without a sufficient break or adequate nourishment. Sometimes these decisions can turn into a life-or-death situation.

Quite a few times my husband and I had rather close brushes with hypothermia. We've always been aware of the early symptoms and been able to take preventive steps before anything drastic has occurred. We've also saved at least half a dozen others who might not have been able to save themselves. When a couple came into the shelter in the Smoky Mountains of North Carolina, wet and shivering, and began to strike wet matches into a totally empty stone fireplace in an attempt to warm themselves, we knew it was time to intercede.

They were fortunate to have others there to save their skins. A hiker needs to be as self-reliant as possible. Hiking promotes this characteristic in a person, although many venture out without the ability or the knowledge to take care of themselves. Taking full responsibility for one's well-being is a scary thing. There are no supports and crutches to fall back on if one does something stupid. A helicopter rescue is costly and will happen only if someone knows you're missing and can send out help.

I read in a newspaper in the desert town of Cabazon, California, about a solo hiker traveling on the Pacific Crest Trail who fell down a cliff and injured his ankle. It was an infrequently used stretch, and he soon grew tired of yelling for help. He lay there for days, writing letters to his loved ones, for he knew he was going to die. Why didn't he crawl to an open spot and start a fire, or signal with a mirror, or lay out a bright piece of clothing? I don't know, but his actions that day—or lack of them—cost him his life.

So with the freedom to go where and when I want also comes the responsibility for my own welfare. To me, it's always been worth it. The thought of what could happen may shake me up and keep me on my toes, but that's good for me, too—it keeps me from getting cocky and having too elevated an opinion of myself.

Whenever a cold front passes and the sky is a brilliant deep blue, the breeze cool and refreshing, and the sun warm, I find myself singing as I hike—with tears in my eyes and a catch in my throat.

There are times, out hiking, when I feel connected to all the life around me: the deer that noses around my camp at twilight because it smells my dinner and is curious; the wind as it plays in my hair; and the evergreens as they swoosh and sway in the breeze. They all feel like my friends, like they know me and want me there. When I lie down at night, my back in close contact with the earth, I can imagine its breath rising and falling. I can look up into the heavens and, with some concentration, tell which way the planet and I are turning in space.

The earth feels alive to me, comfortable and homey—full of acceptance, love, and security, as any good home should make you feel. I don't feel separate from it, nor alienated by it, for it has taught me my most valuable lessons in life, like a good mother. While observing nature, I learned that death is also a part of life, one state of being flowing into the next. The falling leaves, the rotting stump, a rabbit snatched by a hawk's talons to become its supper—all teach me that life changes form, it doesn't disappear. Knowing this helped me to accept both my parents' deaths and to look at dying as natural and necessary.

Hiking over the earth makes me feel a need to take care of it—nurture it. It also makes me heartsick to see the destruction inflicted upon it.

I once took a group of inner-city children out hiking as a favor to a teacher friend. I took them to one of the most beautiful and scenic open ridgewalks and overlooks in the entire state. Some of them complained bitterly. One seventh grader listed out loud all the things she didn't like. "I hate the trees. I hate the rocks. I hate the views." When I asked her why, she said, "Because they're ugly."

That scared me. She was really expressing her discomfort. It didn't feel good to her to be there. This world was unfamiliar and she was filled with hostility. Her discomfort would probably stay with her all her life.

Our children need to care about the earth. They're going to need wild places to run free when their lives—perhaps even more stressful than ours—get the best of them. And they'll certainly need clean water and pure air to sustain their bodies, no matter where they live. How can

Tips

• *You can make a great lantern by placing a candle in an empty tuna can. Perfect for night reading, and it's surprisingly stable. Or stand a flashlight on end and place a one-quart plastic water bottle over it.*

• *To prevent your flashlight from accidently going on in your pack and draining the batteries, use a rubber band to hold the switch in the off position. Or reverse the batteries.*

• *Stand all bottles (stove fuel and water) upright. In camp, keep the fuel bottle outside the tent and when traveling, store it either in an outside pack pocket or in a rock climber's chalk bag tied to your pack. Gas bottles can leak and contaminate clothes and food.*

• *Carry out all trash. Never leave paper in a fire pit for the next person to burn. It looks ugly, may blow away, and can get wet and not burn. Never bury trash or garbage such as chicken bones, because animals will dig it up. On the trail, don't step over those small but noticeable pieces of trash like candy wrappers or chewing gum foil. Pack them out. Carry an extra bag for this purpose.*

• *Before leaving your campsite or lunch spot or rest area, check for articles left behind. Look between rocks where you may have dropped your pocketknife or water bottle or even trash.*

• *Rest every hour or two, even if it's only for five or ten minutes. It's not wasted time—the rest will keep you going farther in the long run.*

• *Give your body a rest on extremely steep terrain without stopping: Pause for a split second on each step while your rear leg is extended behind you and bearing your weight.*

• *Each of the following surfaces can cause injury, so modify your hiking style to prevent problems.*

★Uphill. Walking too fast can cause muscle pulls, heel blisters, Achilles tendinitis, and burnout.

★Downhill. Walking too fast or too slow can cause knee problems, shinsplints, falls, sprained ankles, and toe blisters.

★Level ground. Walking too fast can cause sore feet, especially on rocky surfaces.

you feel affection toward the earth if you don't know it?

Our children, perhaps even more than ourselves, need to get out and play in the woods, in the streams, on the trails, for the future of more than just themselves.

Hiking has made me want to consume less and be less wasteful. When I live with so few material things on the trail, I realize that I actually need very little to survive. Not only are many material goods unnecessary to be happy but they can indeed rob us of that happiness we're hoping they'll provide. They can clutter our lives, suck up our time, cloud our vision, and keep us from the real business of living. They make us hurry. They rob us of our quietness and peace. They steal our lives from us.

Since I've grown closer to nature, I've learned to appreciate some of nature's gifts. Hiking made me appreciate pure water when I had none for 30 miles in the desert. It made me appreciate warmth when I was stuck in a snow storm on Mount Whitney for four days. It made me appreciate people when I was hiking alone. There is nothing like doing without something you really need to make your realize how valuable and important it is in your life, and how everything else is superficial.

Out of all the gifts hiking has given me, perhaps the most important is the responsibility I feel to listen to what the earth has to say. We need to spend time outdoors with it. Leave our buildings behind for a while and our idle jabbering in the city and go out and walk over the land. Listen to the wind. Observe the animals. Watch the day fade and the dawn break. Raise our voices in song. Nature's language is different from man's. There are no words. And it speaks only to those who can hear with their hearts. Once we love the

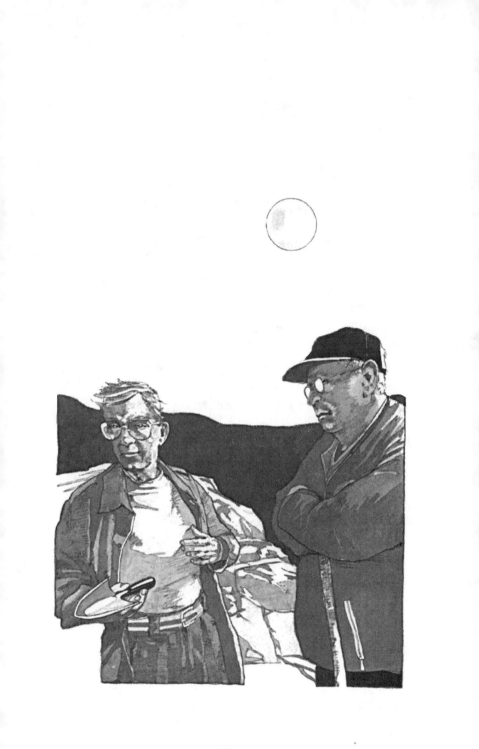

earth, we will not want to harm it. We will not want to poison it. We will respect and take care of it. Is there a better gift for our children and our children's children?

In Pennsylvania, there's a group of retirees who meet each morning at the base of the Blue Mountain near the Appalachian Trail. Armed with loppers, clippers, paint pots, and brushes, they hike anywhere from three to eight miles a day, pruning and trimming as they walk. Affectionately called the Geritol Gang, these senior citizens are the self-appointed guardians of their surrounding woods.

"Too many people retire and six months later they're six feet under," explains Emmitt Francis, their de facto leader. Some of the group have had heart attacks, one has diabetes, and another has cancer that's in remission. They love life, they love the woods and the trail, and they hike to preserve it all.

Fitness was never my main reason for hiking. I went out because I loved being there. As I become older, however, the exercise aspect has become increasingly important. I need exercise in my daily life that I can do no matter where I am, that gives me very little leeway for excuses—and hiking is it.

Hiking helped me stay fit through my pregnancy. It made me feel good at a time when women are likely to feel dumpy, clumsy, and fat. Instead, my toned and strong body gave me a positive self-image and a healthy state of mind. When hundreds of hormones surged through my body in the first trimester, often putting me on an emotional roller coaster, hiking improved my mood and relaxed me.

Heat Exhaustion

To guard against heat exhaustion and heat stroke, consume plenty of water; on hot days, your body can lose about two quarts of fluid per hour. Wear light-colored cotton clothing to reflect the heat. Cotton absorbs moisture from your skin, and, as it evaporates, you feel cooler. Wear sunglasses and a hat with a brim to shade your head. Cool down by dipping your head in a cool stream, or soaking a bandanna and wrapping it around your head.

Early in my fifth month I climbed Mount Katahdin in Maine, the northern terminus of the Appalachian Trail, in celebration of the tenth anniversary of my first journey up the peak. The special people whom I shared the hike with in 1979 were meeting again to retrace our steps up that sacred mountain.

On the top, the wind gusted to 50 mph, and there was little visibility through the thick clouds and rain. We had to pull ourselves up iron handholds in the rock. I couldn't bend my legs into my belly, so my husband often pulled me up with a hand from above, while a friend gave my buttocks a shove from below.

When I stood on the summit and once again ran my finger in the routed sign that said, Springer Mountain, Georgia, 2,100 miles, I relived the joy I had experienced on my journey years before. And I felt even greater joy as I reached beneath my Windbreaker and rubbed my belly and my baby and thought of all the wonderful walks we would share in the future.

Now that our second child has arrived, we will have to put our long hikes on hold for a while. Every few years, Todd and I like to get out on the trail for a few months and dust out the cobwebs in our arteries and in our heads. Perhaps even more important than our physical health is what hiking does for our mental well-being.

Whenever Todd and I have a problem in our lives that we can't seem to solve, we always take it out for a hike. It's so much easier to talk when we're walking. The motion of my body sets my mind in motion, too. Thoughts don't seem as jumbled or confused, and, after a

Blisters

If the weather is warm and your load heavy, take your boots and socks off frequently for ten- to fifteen-minute breaks. It will feel marvelous and will help keep your feet dry; moisture causes blisters.

The first sign of a developing blister is a hot and tender spot, so take action immediately and apply moleskin before it gets to the full-blown stage.

If a blister develops, draining it will increase comfort and hasten healing. Puncture the skin with a sterilized needle (hold the needle over a match). Let the fluid drain, apply an antibiotic cream, then cover with a nonstick bandage. Put moleskin or Second Skin (available at drug stores in the foot-care section) over the bandage.

while, reason and clarity seem to flow out with my words.

Every now and then, spaces come between Todd and me—mostly when we are intensely involved in separate projects and our energies are going in different directions. We plan a hike then, to center ourselves and get back in touch with what is most important—our relationship. With no other distractions around, it's easier to do. We always come home more in love and more sensitive and understanding of each other. *Solvitor Ambulado*—it is solved by walking.

A long hike is often beneficial in mental healing for there is so much time to think and sort out feelings. There are folks who are on the trail just for that reason. They are in transition: recovering from a divorce, accepting a death, finishing school and getting ready to enter the work world, or abandoning their former occupation because they're dissatisfied and empty.

Long-distance hiking can help me set my priorities in a more realistic order, because my daily activities are trimmed down and simplified. What is really necessary in life becomes obvious, and what I as an individual need to be happy becomes more clear.

At one of my last town stops on the Appalachian Trail, I learned I had lost my full scholarship from art school. I walked back from the post office teary-eyed, but shortly afterward, as we climbed out of the gorge, I started thinking. "I could go to art school and spend the rest of my life learning how to paint, but there comes a time when I must start doing what I love."

I had my first solo art show when I returned and painted scenes along the trail, and it was a huge success.

Trail Pointers

- *Extend your days. Start before or at sunrise to gain flexibility during the day. You'd be surprised how many miles you can do by starting at sunrise and hiking until sunset.*

- *Enhance your trip by identifying birds, trees, insects, and flowers along the way. A small guidebook may be worth its weight. A lightweight pair of binoculars or a monocular can help you to see and identify birds and small animals. Carry them, and other often-needed items like sunscreen, in a front fannypack.*

- *Stay flexible. For instance, camping near water is usually what most backpackers aim for, but suppose you want to pitch your tent on a summit or open ridge where no water is available? Instead of carrying cooking and drinking water all day, try fixing your evening meal at lunchtime when water is available. Then your lunch items can be eaten for supper at the end of the day when you only need drinking water.*

- *If you get lost, some natural signs showing direction can come in handy: 1. Snow is generally more granular on southern slopes. 2. Evergreens are bushiest on the eastern side. 3. The tops of pines and hemlocks point east. 4. Vegetation is larger and more open on northern slopes, smaller and denser on southern slopes.*

Contrary to what my family used to think, we can hike trails all of our lives. If that's what brings us the most joy, then that's what we must do.

I hike because of how it makes me feel and because of the person I become: happy, peaceful, centered, and whole. What better reason do I need for doing what I love?

The shelter was packed with nineteen men, stuffed in like sardines, sleeping bag to sleeping bag, from one end of the three-sided log shelter to the other. Colleen and I pulled in around dusk, after our first day on the Appalachian Trail. It was clear there was no room at the inn. But even after a day of rain we cheerfully accepted the fact that we would have to set up our tarp outside. A more immediate concern than shelter, however, was tending to our stomachs. We went behind the shelter and pulled out the once-frozen steaks we had brought from home to celebrate our journey's kickoff. For some moronic reason, during an entire year of laborious planning, we had never attempted to light our new backpacking stove. At least we were smart enough to bring along the manufacturer's directions. After a few false tries, we finally got our meat sizzling. While the steaks cooked, we pulled out some colored photos that I had cut from equipment catalogs showing different ways a tarp could be set up. We had never set it up before we left, either.

We felt pretty foolish and pretty green. As the light faded, one of the men in the shelter came around back and invited us in. They had made room. Two hikers had tiny, lightweight hammocks that they strung from the rafters, opening up two spaces on the floor. "Feel free to eat your supper here, too," he encouraged. "Sure smells good." Colleen and I passed around our pot with the steak bones and they took turns chewing on the fat.

Because of our enthusiasm and good fortune, we kept on going. That isn't usually the case, however. Some folks think hiking—unlike sports like whitewater canoeing and rock climbing—is such an easy and casual activity, and that anyone can go out there and do fine. After all, it's "only walking." And so every year about 1,000 hiking hopefuls head down to Springer Mountain, Georgia, to the start of the AT, to begin what will be to most, the adventure of a lifetime. But by the time six months are up, only about 100 of them will have reached their goal. The rest will have fallen by the wayside. Many will return home during the first few weeks. Some will make it only up the approach trail and turn around at the sign announcing the start of the trail. Every year the *Appalachian Trailway News* magazine runs want ads stating: tent, $10, used once; sleeping bag, $10, used once; set of AT guidebooks, $10, used once. What happens? Why do so many abandon their journey when they have planned and dreamed about it for so many years? Many go out with a romantic, unrealistic view of long-distance hiking and are disappointed when the demands of the trail contradict their expectations.

Life outdoors requires good measures of common sense and backwoods skills. There are many people who merely went out for a walk, but instead died of exposure. Even in the summer, if certain conditions are present— chilly air, cool rain, fatigue, lack of nourishment, or wet clothes—a hiker can die. There are basics that must be practiced to prevent an uncomfortable situation from developing into a dangerous one: stopping to eat before one gets too hungry, resting before exhaustion, putting on warm clothes when it's cold and rain gear before getting wet. Most decisions involve common sense, but some good sound backwoods wisdom can go a long way. Get a good book like Colin Fletcher's *The New Complete Walker III* and study it. Go out hiking and backpacking often to feel comfortable in all situations and weather.

Less important than common sense and experience is equipment. Buy the best you can afford and know how to use it. But though equipment is necessary, it's not what ultimately gets you down the trail. There was a man who hiked the AT with a golf bag as a backpack, and several people have walked hundreds of miles barefoot on the AT. What you do choose to purchase and bring along should fit your body and your needs well.

It helps to be in good physical shape, but conditioning does not always ensure success. JoAnn, my AT partner, never really used her body to exercise before her journey, and didn't feel strong until she covered 500 miles, but she still managed to complete her goal. Most times, unless you have a heart condition, your body will tell you when enough is enough, if you listen to it. I met a young man on the AT down in Georgia who had run ten miles every day in preparation for his hike. His cardiovascular system was strong, all right—so strong that he motored up and down those incredibly steep mountains with ease. Because he never felt winded, he thought he could push his body with a backpack on. What he didn't realize was that run-

Equipment

• *Purchase quality backpacking equipment from a reputable supplier. Quality gear will hold up better in the long run, and should you have problems, the manufacturer will often replace the damaged item.*

• *Freshen your sleeping bag and tent before your trip by putting both in the sun to air. Turn them frequently to prevent sun damage. When you return home, air them again. Tents and bags must be thoroughly dry before packing, because mildew can easily ruin them. Even if it doesn't rain during your trip, they will probably collect condensation.*

• *Select plastic water bottles with wide mouths. The wide opening makes it easier for cleaning, spooning out the contents, and removing partially frozen water. They're also simpler to fill in a stream. Get a clear one so you can see how much water is left.*

• *Carry a water bag. A nylon bladder bag lets you avoid repeated trips to the spring and, when filled, it makes a great pillow, or you can lay it in the sun to warm and then take a pleasant shower.*

• *Consider including a Frisbee. It's light and fun to toss in camp. In a pinch, a clean Frisbee can double as a plate or washbowl.*

• *Everyone has his own packing system, but in general, place heavy items as close to your back as you can. Bulky gear like your tent and food supplies should be on top. Your sleeping bag is a good item for the bottom of the pack, and your clothes should go somewhere in between. If you have an internal-frame pack, pad sharp objects because they'll invariably poke you in the back.*

• *Protect maps and guidebooks by carrying them in a heavy, self-sealing, plastic Ziploc bag or plastic map case. When it's raining, position the map face up so you don't have to open the bag and unfold the map every time you need to consult it. You can also seal maps in clear contact paper.*

• *Put pack pockets to good use. In an outside pocket, keep items you'll use often during the day, such as rain gear, sunglasses, toilet paper, and maps.*

• *Losing gear on the trail, or leaving it behind, can be a problem, since every item in your pack has a purpose. To reduce chances of this happening, leave the pocket zipper or flap on your pack open after removing something. Before shouldering your pack again, check for open pockets and make sure everything has been replaced.*

ning works different muscles than hiking with a backpack. He injured his kneecap so badly that a plastic one had to be inserted, and he was never able to backpack again. Working the *right* muscles is very important. Ideally, the best way to prepare for backpacking simply is to backpack—to put on a loaded pack and walk up and down on uneven surfaces.

You can learn a lot about success and failure by looking at those individuals who have hiked long distances.

I have been actively involved in the Appalachian Long Distance Hikers Association since its founding in 1981. I have held the position of coordinator and assistant coordinator, and know hundreds of long-distance hikers. I've also taught backpacking at a local college for five years. I've seen a lot of successes, but even more failures. From my experience, I'd have to say that most of the reasons are psychological, not physical ones. I say this in part because some of the most extraordinary hikers I have known have overcome major physical handicaps and accomplished what so few even attempt.

Watching Bob Barker coming down the trail (white-haired, huge pack towering over his head, clipping along on crutches!) makes you realize there are few excuses in life if the desire is strong enough.

Bob, who was stricken with multiple sclerosis in 1970, knows his muscles will deteriorate if he doesn't use them. He has hiked the AT three times, all since the age of sixty-five, and has been known to cover up to thirty miles a day.

Then there's Bill Irwin, the first blind man to complete

the entire AT, with the help of his Seeing Eye dog, Orient. The pair managed to scale cliffs, cross raging rivers, avoid snakes and bears, and scramble over boulder fields for 2,100 miles. Orient watched Bill's right foot with his right eye. If there was something on the trail that Bill would fall over, Orient would take a step and wait, thus indicating a hazard. Bill would find it by swinging his ski pole hiking staff. At trail intersections, Orient used the scent of hikers who had gone before to decide which way to turn. After a while, some hikers even caught Orient actually looking at the white paint blazes on the trees that mark the way.

Why were these two men successful? For starters, they both know that success depends on mental toughness and the ability to withstand the hardships of the trail. A good attitude and a burning passion mean more than strong muscles. It usually takes only a few weeks of steady hiking to get your body accustomed to the exercise. After that, it's mostly up to your head to keep you going.

Before you set off on your hike, make sure your expectations aren't unrealistic. Hiking and backpacking can be thought of very romantically, when in reality there's a lot to contend with. Warren Doyle, eight-time AT end-to-ender and creator of the Appalachian Trail Institute—a program designed to give an honest, realistic idea of what's involved in hiking from Georgia to Maine—had this to say: "Don't whine about things you can't control. If things get hard, accept it with good humor. If things get easy, don't take your good fortune for granted, but appreciate and exult in it. Don't blame your discomfort on the trail or the weather. Look at

yourself for not being able to adapt."

Many people try to fight the trail or the weather or the heat or the bugs. But you have to be able to flow with whatever is handed out to you. You can't make a mountain any less steep, so don't waste energy complaining. You have to adapt your mind, heart, and soul to the terrain. Undesirable conditions can crop up on a short weekend hike. The secret to your success and to the amount of pleasure you derive from a hike ultimately depends on your attitude.

Interestingly, much of the same applies to everyday life. Learn these lessons on the trail, and your daily life will be richer and more satisfying, too.

Warren suggests you get used to a lower comfort level than at home. You don't need a change of clean clothing every day you're on the trail. You don't need a daily shower either. You can live without your make-up, mousse, hair dryers, shavers, and deodorant. Hikers talk about the "dirty fingernail syndrome"—the initial discomfort they feel from getting dirty—but most get beyond this and sometimes even enjoy not having to deal with all the niceties of staying neat and clean. It frees them for other, more important activities—like rock sunning by a stream or hawk watching on an open pinnacle.

When everything is said and done, the most important words to remember are those of Nessmuk, the old mountain man from Pennsylvania: "We don't go out there to rough it. We go out there to smooth it. We get it rough enough at home."

Have fun. Keep a light heart. Take your time.

THE HIKER'S WORLD

Trails in America

America is blessed with a vast network of foot trails and roads, used by millions of hikers, cyclists, and wilderness lovers. Trails were part of America long before the white man arrived. American Indians traveled vast distances on trails, many of which are still in use. The pioneers migrated westward on wagon trails, and again, many of these are part of the present trail system.

Modern trail building began toward the end of the eighteenth century. In the 1860s, the Sierra Nevada Mountains were explored and mapped. Near the end of the decade a young botanist, John Muir, arrived in the Sierra Nevadas. He had planned to stay for only a few months before heading off to the Amazon for field studies, but because he was penniless he took a job as a shepherd's assistant. The job brought him to Yosemite Valley, California, and literally changed his life and the history of the American wilderness.

Yosemite became the love of Muir's life: "I have run wild," he wrote. "As long as I live, I'll hear waterfalls, and birds and winds sing. I'll interpret the rocks, learn the language of the floods, storm, and avalanche. I'll acquaint myself with the glaciers and wild gardens, and get as near the heart of the world as I can."

Muir was a visionary. He knew the glorious Yosemite Valley and the Sierra Nevadas needed to be protected, and he took it upon himself to publicize the message of conservation to the world. His words in the *New York Tribune* and other prominent publications encouraged everyone with "the right manners of the wilderness to come and explore, and hence, permanently protect its wild beauty." He believed that "if people in general could be got into the woods, even for once, to hear the trees speak for themselves, all difficulties in the way of forest preservation would vanish."

Muir's ideas took root, and in 1892, in San Francisco, he and a handful of other people interested in making the Sierra more accessible and better known founded the Sierra Club. Many of the club's charter members were scientists, and exploring, mapping, and photographing the mountains became the first priority of the new organization.

For the first nine years, the Sierra Club had no recreational outings, unlike the Appalachian Mountain Club in the White Mountains of New Hampshire and the Mazamas in Oregon—two other early hiking organizations. However, in 1901 the Sierra Club's Board of Directors decided to institute an annual summer outing.

These organized hikes were major excursions, consisting of between one and two hundred people. Camping equipment was transported by wagon and then later by mule train, and meals were prepared by a commissary. Sierra Club outings were never simply hiking trips. Campers were advised to read Muir's *The Mountains of California,* and Le Conte's *Ramblings Through the High Sierra* to better prepare themselves for the excursion. Once the trip was underway, there were lectures on forestry and the history of Yosemite. Muir himself spoke on geomorphology, the study of earth's terrain. Culture was also served with poetry readings, violin concerts, and plays written, produced, and performed exclusively for the outings.

The early Sierra Club members opened new routes and developed a system of trails that improved access to the Sierra's backcountry. By the early 1930s, most of the high country was accessible.

Female Sierra Club members joined the first

hike, although the Sierra Club issued them specific advice on dress: "Skirts can be short, not more than half way from knee to ankle, and under them can be worn shorter dark colored bloomers."

By 1901, the date of the first Sierra Club hike, the high mountains were considered safe enough for female hikers, who were expected to hike twenty miles a day and keep pace with their male companions. These early women hikers were mostly Berkeley and Stanford girls, and they easily kept pace; it was written that "their vigor and endurance was a revelation to all."

About that time, hiker and mountaineer Annie Smith Peck was making a name for herself. This adventurous woman was born of a cultured, well-to-do family of distinguished ancestry, and appeared as the epitome of a Victorian scholar. Life completely changed for her, however, when she visited the Alps at age thirty-five and wrote, "In beholding this majestic, awe-inspiring peak (Matterhorn) I felt that I should never be truly happy until I, too, should scale those frowning walls which have beckoned so many upwards, a few to their own destruction."

When Peck successfully scaled the Matterhorn in 1895, she joined the roster of great alpinists and gained overnight fame. Peck was the first woman to wear pants (knickerbockers) for climbing, at a time when all other ladies wore floor-length skirts for even the most energetic outings. Her costume was topped with a felt hat that resembled a plate, tied on with a veil. She climbed mountains until she was seventy-five years old, including the historic first ascent of 22,205-foot Mount Huascaran in Peru. She remains a powerful encouragement to women climbers everywhere.

While Peck was scaling mountains and the Sierra was being opened up to hikers, trail construction was also moving apace in the eastern states.

The Long Trail in Vermont, which stretches 225 miles from the Massachusetts border to Canada, opened in 1910. A visionary similar to Muir was Benton MacKaye, a Harvard-educated forester, philosopher, and regional planner, who envisioned the "Appalachian Domain"—a continuous trail following the backbone of the Appalachian Mountain Range, formed by tying together existing trails and creating hundreds of miles of new ones. He saw the trail as a place where people laboring away in cities could find a true respite for body and spirit, just as they do today. MacKaye hoped the AT would offset what he saw as the "negative effect on mankind of rapid mechanization and urbanization."

Clarence Stein, one of the AT's early promoters said, "Workers' homes are congested, in undesirable neighborhoods; parks are inadequate; cities are devouring farms and forests; it is as though man had been created for industry and not industry to serve man's needs. . . . We need the sweep of hills or sea as tonic for our jaded nerves." The Appalachian Trail came into being in 1937, just a decade and a half after the first stretch was built in 1922 in New York State.

Eleven years later, Pennsylvanian Earl Shaffer became the first person to hike its entire more than two-thousand-mile length uninterrupted, during a four-month backpacking trip. It was a considerable accomplishment. Maintenance on the trail had lapsed considerably during World War II, while many trail workers were active in the armed services. Storm damage, logging operations, and natural growth had erased much of the treadway, and the markings were faded or gone. But like Benton MacKaye, Earl Shaffer had a dream. He longed "to walk the army out of my system, both mentally and physically." Shouldering his heavy and bulky canvas rucksack, and wearing his "Birdshooter" boots, he moved north with the spring to successfully arrive on Mount Katahdin in Maine on August 5, 1948.

Emma Gatewood (Grandma Gatewood) became the first woman to hike the entire AT in one continuous stretch in 1955, at the age of sixty-seven. She hiked in sneakers and laid her body down at night on a plastic shower curtain. The Appalachian Trail Conference commented: "It is hoped that no one will follow her example with respect to lack of preparedness, experience, and equipment." They came around though and gave Grandma the respect she deserved, for she went on to hike the AT *two more times* in her hiking career.

By the late '60s and early '70s, hiking and backpacking increased throughout the entire country. Lightweight gear entered the market and new periodicals such as *Backpacker* magazine appeared. Young people were drawn to the outdoors by a renewed love of nature, but perhaps the most important factor was the passing of the National Trails Act in 1968. The Act designated two national scenic trails: the Appalachian Trail—the only completed marked footpath—and the Pacific Crest Trail—a 2,600-mile trail from Mexico to Canada that has only a few signs and no blazes to speak of. The National Park Service, through the Secretary of the Interior, was given principal responsibility for the Appalachian National Scenic Trail. The route was fixed, maps, and trail descriptions were published, and the long process of acquiring the privately owned corridor lands began. It was not until 1978 that President Jimmy Carter signed the Appalachian Trail Bill, which authorized funds for a private corridor protecting the trail.

In 1984, the National Park Service Director signed over to the Appalachian Trail Conference the responsibility for managing the trail corridor and maintaining the footpath itself. This was a milestone in trail history, because, for the first time, extensive public lands were entrusted to a private organization. Secretary of the Interior William P. Clark pointed to this development as evidence that volunteers can do a job equal to if not better than a federal agency. To date, only a handful of miles of the AT remain unsecured, but efforts continue to acquire adjacent buffer lands and protect "viewsheds" to preserve the trail experience.

Following in the Appalachian Trail's footsteps, volunteers are building trails all over the country, attempting to put our eight national scenic trails and countless smaller ones on the land—and not just on the maps. □

Cold Weather Food

I once met a backpacker out on a summer trip who had no food except for some wild green apples he had found in an abandoned orchard. He got away with this because in mild weather most people in reasonably good shape aren't hurt by a little hunger and weight loss.

Winter, however, is a different story. Strenuous exercise, coupled with severe weather, can drain your stamina and make you more prone to frostbite, hypothermia, and other injuries. What you eat can make the difference. When it's cold outside, think of food as fuel for heat, energy, and survival.

The effects of cold can hit unexpectedly. On several winter trips I have found myself ravenously hungry after merely lying in my sleeping bag for a few hours following a hearty dinner. I hadn't been exercising; my body simply used all that food just trying to keep warm. Strenuous exercise would have only compounded the problem. A winter activity will burn 12 percent more calories and 32 percent more fat than the same exercise done in warmer conditions.

As far as caloric requirements go, 3,000 to 4,000 calories a day will usually suffice for warm-weather backpacking; in cold weather, push that to around 6,000. Maybe you've noticed that, on an extended winter trip, it is nearly impossible to carry enough food to supply you with large amounts of calories. Even many high-mileage, long-distance summer hikers are continuously hungry because they do not have the pack capacity to carry all the food they need. But it is possible, with a little knowledge and planning, to ensure a safe and enjoyable trip where the bears do the growling and your stomach doesn't.

Keep two things in mind: nutrition and calories. Proteins and fats release energy over a long period of time, which makes them particularly important during long-term, strenuous activities. A piece of chocolate (carbohydrate) will give you a quick power boost for that last mountain of the day, but a hunk of cheese or a handful of jerky (fat and protein) will fuel you through a longer, less strenuous period. Proteins and fats also take a lot of energy to digest, especially at high altitudes, so they should not be eaten in large amounts before or while you're working hard. Spread them out throughout your day. A liberal use of butter in hot cereal and during suppers is a good way to boost your fat intake. Dump extra powdered milk and cheese into meals to increase your protein.

Most of your calories, though, should come from relatively "instant-energy" carbohydrates, preferably complex carbohydrates like grains, pastas, instant potatoes, and dried fruits. To add extra calories and nutrients, pad your menu with foods like sunflower seeds, nuts, and raisins in your oatmeal. Drink instant soup or hot chocolate instead of tea or coffee. Buy tuna in oil instead of spring water. The water you use to cook your pasta is loaded with starch and carbohydrates, so use it in your meal (in soups and sauces, for instance) instead of discarding it. Consider the calorie-to-weight ratio of all your foods and select only those with the most calories for the least amount of weight. There is no room for "empty" food on a winter trip. Leave the featherweight sugarless drink mixes and desserts at home.

Because water is often hard to find on winter trips, it helps to use foods that already contain their moisture. For dessert, feast on cookies instead of instant pudding. On extended trips, canned foods or frozen homemade stews in sealed, boilable bags can cut down on water use. On longer trips, supplement meals with freeze-dried foods that take less water, require little or no cooking time, and are lightweight and compact. Rice takes less water to prepare than noodles, and skinny noodles take less fuel to cook than wide ones. One-pot meals keep hotter longer than multipart entrees and offer fewer packages for cold fingers to open and fewer dishes to clean.

I don't recommend eating snow to satisfy your thirst; it lowers your body temperature and you expend extra energy—though you may not notice—to bring it back up.

Your stove is one of the most important pieces of equipment on a winter backpacking trip. Cut a small square of closed-cell foam pad to put under your stove when cooking to insulate it from the cold ground and decrease heat conduction. Although it's a good idea to sleep with your stove gear anyway—to keep it warm and ready for firing—white gas models will survive the abuse of cold better than others, such as the more limited butane models, which won't work at all below 20° F.

In hot weather, you cannot ignore your thirst; it's as apparent as the sweat running down your back. Cold weather, however, masks thirst, probably because your primary concern is warmth and the environment is so far removed from the typically "thirsty" landscape and searing heat. Lack of water in cold weather makes you drink less, and rapidly breathing dry, cold air quickly dehydrates you. Dehydration can increase your risk of frostbite because your blood volume, your primary heat conductor, is actually reduced.

Tank up every time you come across running water. Drink plenty of hot drinks before and after meals to ensure consumption of that much-needed five quarts a day. When you're chilled, drink and eat hot foods to help your body warm itself. Be sure to keep liquids available at all times.

To keep your water supplies from freezing at night, sleep with the tightly closed, leakproof bottles in your sleeping bag. Choose wide-mouth containers that resist icing over. To prevent freezing during the day, cut and fit closed-cell foam pads around your water bottles as insulation. Glue the seams with contact cement. Alcohol, often said to be a warming beverage, does create the impression of warmth by its bite and by temporarily increasing blood flow to your extremities. But this only serves to rob your body core of much-needed heat and, on the whole, drops your body temperature. Avoid caffeine, too, which constricts blood vessels.

Everyone reacts differently to cold, depending on metabolism, body size, gender, normal body temperature, and health. Smaller people have more body surface for their weight than bigger people, so they lose heat more easily. Women's body temperatures run three to four degrees lower than men's, and their hands and feet are more prone to feeling cold earlier.

Of particular importance to women is the role iron plays in resisting cold. Iron assists the formation of hemoglobin, an oxygen-carrier important for heat-producing processes. A deficiency in iron can alter thyroid metabolism, which regulates body heat. Because most women are iron deficient, they should consider taking iron supplements. You can also add foods like molasses, wheat germ, and apricots to a winter backpacking diet to boost iron intake. Take vitamin C-rich foods simultaneously to enhance iron absorption. Because your body is coldest between 3 A.M. and 5 A.M., take a high-iron, high-calorie snack to bed with you in case you wake up hungry and cold.

When it comes down to it, aside from the peace and stark beauty of the winter landscape, cold-weather backpacking is one of the few times you can eat a lot, run clear off the caloric chart, and not gain weight or feel guilty. That, in itself, is a treat! □

Dehydrating Food

Planning your trip will require a considerable amount of time. But a few extra hours dehydrating your own food will be time well spent. You can prepare some of the healthiest, most economical, and most satisfying backcountry meals with minimal effort.

Dehydrating foods is the simple process of removing most of the water under low heat (105° to 115° F). This lightens the food and retains much of the natural flavor. To do it right, you'll need a dehydrator. It can be home-built, or you can buy a countertop model with a thermostat. Your local health food store might sell them, or you can buy good ones from Harvest Maid Dehydrators (4064 Peavey Rd., Chaska, MN 55318, tel.: 612/448-4400). Prices range from $80 to $170. The same units can be bought from Sears, J.C. Penney, and Burpee Seed Catalogs. Another good model is the Harvest Savor Dehydrator from Vita-Mix (Dept. BP0289-P, 8615 Usher Rd., Cleveland, OH 44138, tel.: 216/235-4840). Their units sell from $100 to $130.

To help certain foods (brown rice, kidney beans for chili and pintos for refried beans) rehydrate quicker on the trail, I cook them before drying. To eliminate cans, I dry the white meat of chicken, turkey, ham (with no water added), ground lean burger, and institution-size cans of water packed tuna. Avoid fatty meats like dark poultry and pork because the oils quickly turn rancid.

You can dry sauces, thick soups and pureed fruits by first putting plastic wrap on your dehydrator trays. Just about any meal you enjoy at home can be dehydrated.

You might want to steam-blanch fruits before drying to destroy microbes and further retard spoilage. To blanch, use a large kettle with a couple of inches of boiling water. Suspend but don't immerse a wire mesh basket of clean, diced fruits in the kettle. Cover. Once steam starts escaping, blanch for two minutes. Remove from the kettle and immerse the fruit in cold water to halt heating action. Spread the pieces on a cloth and blot dry.

When you place fruit on drying trays, make sure there's enough space between the pieces to ensure even heat penetration. Since dryer times vary with dryer and type of fruit, test pieces occasionally. The fruit is ready when it is leathery and can be cut without seeping residual moisture.

Dry vegetables the same way, except always blanch two to five minutes before dehydrating.

Pasteurization, a mild heat treatment, improves the safety and shelf life of dehydrated fruits and veggies. Two weeks after drying, reheat the foods at 175° F. Heat fruit for fifteen minutes and vegetables for ten minutes, then portion and pack for storage.

I store my dried foods in brown-paper lunch bags. The paper keeps out light and doesn't react with the food (as might occur with some plastics). On each bag I write the contents and the drying date. Then I put them in thick resealable plastic bags. To reduce trail cooking time, soak the evening meal in water while setting up camp.

You can expect properly dried dehydrated food to have a shelf life of several years. And with the money you save, you can plan another trip. For more information consult the book *Dry It—You'll Like It!* by Gen MacManiman (P.O. Box 546, Fall City, WA 98024, tel.: 206/222-5587). □

Bears

A half-dozen times a night I force my eyes open and peer through the tent door at our hanging food bags. Moonlight shows them still swaying gently in the High Sierra breeze. Bear watch. The job is mine, for I'm the lightest sleeper. It doesn't make for the most restful sleep after a hard day's backpacking, but I'd rather keep my belly full.

"IT'S HERE!" I yell, as a heavy movement of tree branches wakes me. My hiking companions are well-conditioned: Their eyes shoot open, they throw off their sleeping bags, unzip their tents, grab the rocks piled by the door, and zing the bear in the rump. In a matter of seconds, he clambers down the tree and scuttles out of sight.

In national parks, keeping your food away from bears is the law, with violations punishable by fines up to $500 or even imprisonment. In 1988, this law became a challenge in the western mountains. Nuisance bear activity reached exceptional levels because the second-straight year of drought reduced the bears' natural food supply.

Black bears *(Ursus americanus)* are widespread throughout the Appalachians, Rockies, and

Sierra. They will eat anything you do. They are intelligent and learn quickly. When they repeatedly obtain food or garbage, the rewards overwhelm their natural fear of people, and they can become quite persistent thieves. If a bear turns destructive and potentially dangerous, it will be destroyed by park authorities. But the bears are park residents, and we are only visitors; it's our responsibility to keep the bears from becoming problems.

The counterbalance hanging technique keeps most black bears and other wildlife from enjoying your meals before you do. For seasoned campground bears, it only buys you time. The technique involves two food sacks of equal weight hanging in balance over the end of a high tree branch. It sounds simple but takes practice.

Counterbalance starts with your campsite choice; tree availability, not access to water or aesthetics, determines the site. You'll need to make camp early because you'll need to eat, clean up, and still have enough daylight to play the food-hanging game. Try it with a flashlight and you'll need an extra large helping of skill, patience, and good humor.

Besides food, hang everything that holds odors: shampoo, soap, insect repellent, sunscreen, water bottles that held drink mix, and so on.

(Fang marks in my plastic first aid box serve as my constant reminder.) Don't forget about wooden spoons, the pot scrubber, all garbage, and snacks stored in fannypacks. Leave your empty pack on the ground with the top flap and packets open so the bear won't tear it apart during his search. Store water bottles out of sight since bears will test any container.

Ideally the sacks shouldn't exceed ten pounds, but on an extended trip that may be impossible. The heavier the bags, the more difficult counterbalance hanging becomes. A carabiner helps fasten multiple drawcords together and eliminates knots, which often come loose. The trick comes in getting both bags the same distance from the ground. Weight the bags evenly and adjust their hanging height with a long stick.

After completing your best hang job, set up the tent a few yards away from the suspended sacks, but not directly underneath; you don't want to find bear and sacks in bed with you if they fall. Position a tent window in direct view of the hanging food. Your close proximity will do nothing to keep bears away, but it will help you hear them arrive, especially if it's windy or there's a creek nearby.

Assemble an arsenal of small rocks by each tent's exit—more than a few, because repeated night raids are common. Arrange your (clean!) cook gear around the base of the tree and on the ground below the sacks as a burglar alarm. The clanging metal should waken you before the sound of food bags hitting the ground does. Put the lightest sleeper by the window or door, and sleep with one ear open.

All this might sound pretty bearproof, but these camp robbers can be surprisingly ingenious. If the branch is too strong, a bear can walk out and pull up your rope or chew it until the sacks drop. If the limb is too springy, bears can bounce sacks off the end. A mother might send a cub out to retrieve the loot. And if the branch is just right, the bear could pull a stunt like the one in Yosemite did to me: He climbed the tree, jumped on the limb, and fell to the ground. Then he repeated the process until the limb weakened and broke, sending bear, sacks, and branch crashing down. If a bear does score, remember that it's your responsibility to clean up his mess.

If it's beginning to sound like you can't win, then you're finally getting the picture. Carla Neasel, one of five Yosemite rangers hired to roam the park's backcountry and educate visitors on proper food storage, says, "Consider hanging your food as a delaying tactic only. It merely buys you enough time to get up and act." Even

Carla has had her food stolen by bears.

In the high country the absence of suitable bear-bagging trees poses an added challenge. One ranger suggested, and we successfully tried, suspending our food over a rock by jamming the cordlock into a crack reached from above. You could hang it off a ledge safe enough for nimble humans but not clumsy bears.

Another time we put our bags in a rock opening on the ground and piled boulders on top, then our pots and pans; we called it our "masonry cache with the stainless-steel alarm system." It worked great against bears, but smaller critters got inside and chewed a few things.

A high-priority project for the National Park Service is testing and evaluating portable bearproof food canisters. Durt-ty Business (Garcia Machine, 14097 Avenue 272, Visalia, California 93277; tel.: 209/732-3785) sells one that holds six hundred cubic inches. Unfortunately for weight-conscious backpackers, the $75 canister is fairly heavy—almost four pounds.

Individual parks with varying bear species and behavior advise different treatment when confronting robber bears. In 1987, Yosemite, Sequoia, and Kings Canyon National Parks adopted a "mild aggression" policy, in which they encouraged campers to bang pots, yell, and throw objects in hopes of restoring the black bears' natural, human-avoiding behavior. One bit of advice: Never aim at a bear's face because a direct facial hit might provoke an angry charge. Throw to sting, not to injure.

Grizzly bears *(Ursus arctos horribilis)* are a different story. In grizzly country food storage is more complicated and crucial. Use freeze-dried food, which has minimal odor. If possible, do not sleep in the same clothes that you cooked and ate in; hang them with your food. Put all food and garbage in sealed plastic bags before loading and hanging stuff sacks. Sleep upwind from your kitchen area and hang sacks so food odors do not waft over you.

Rangers at griz-country parks don't advocate counterbalancing. Since adult grizzlies cannot climb trees—although grizzly cubs can, and the adults can "climb" up branches to obtain food— they advise suspending food between two trees, ten feet from the ground and four feet from each tree. Check with NPS before venturing into grizzly backcountry for more specific instructions on dealing with these unpredictable bruins. ☐

Water

- Drink a minimum of three to four quarts of water a day, especially in winter when you don't feel as thirsty as you do in summer.
- Drink cool, not icy, water. In cold weather you can get chilled gulping large quantities of cold water too fast.
- If your urine is darker than normal, you're not drinking enough. If you're not urinating often, you're not drinking enough and you run the risk of becoming dehydrated. That's why it's important to drink often!
- In sub-zero weather carry water bottles in a pocket near you or buried deep in your pack so the water won't freeze. A wool sock pulled over the bottle also offers some protection. At night, screw the lids on tight and set your bottles upside down, so that if ice does form, it can't plug the pouring end.
- Keep your bottle full. If water is in short supply on a winter trip, top it off with a bit of snow after each drink.
- When melting snow over your camp stove, have an inch or so of starter water in the pan, then slowly add snow. Use icy, crusty snow or the wettest snow available.
- Be wary of pink or yellow snow.

Watermelon snow gets its name from the color, taste, and scent caused by microorganisms that can bring on diarrhea.

• Melt and warm clean snow in your mouth before swallowing it.

• A spring where you can actually see the water bubbling out of the ground is the safest place to get drinking water. To filter out particles of soil, use a bandanna stretched over your water bottle. Push the fabric down to form a funnel.

• Besides removing particles from the water, you'll need to eliminate *Giardia lamblia,* which contaminates water sources and is carried by humans and animals. Ingest as few as ten or twenty of the protozoa and you may become sick, because they multiply in your intestines. Symptoms usually show within a week or two and include stomach cramps, diarrhea, bloating, loss of appetite, and vomiting. Some people show no symptoms, but remain carriers for months or years. If you think you have been infected, get treatment with antibiotics.

Eliminate giardiasis by boiling, filtering, and treating water with chemicals.

• If you know water will be scarce, drink as much as you can before you start out.

• Bury water. Because snow is a good insulator,

a lidded pot of water buried a foot or so in the snow will remain unfrozen overnight. Mark the spot carefully. If you're staying in one camp for several nights, bury the pot in different locations each night, because snowmelt around the pot produces ice.

• If you have to melt snow for water, you'll need to carry considerably more fuel, which, like water, weighs about two pounds per quart. You also must allow more time for meal preparations. In a brisk, cold wind, it can take an hour and a stoveful of fuel to melt and boil just one quart of water.

• Camp near water if possible, but at least two hundred feet from lakes and streams. And wash at least one hundred feet from water sources. Use biodegradable soaps.

• If your itinerary rules out the possibility of camping near water, be sure to tank up while you're traveling. Fill up all bottles at the last running water source before a dry camp.

• Clean your water bottle regularly. The threads are prime breeding ground for mold and bacteria that can cause dysentery, especially if you use powdered drink mixes. □

HIKING FOR
TOMORROW

From behind, she looked like any other long-distance hiker on the Appalachian Trail. Her calves were strong and muscular. They pumped and relaxed with each climbing step. Her huge pack rode above her head, stuffed with supplies for her next week in the woods. I was gaining on her, but only because my back carried a measly day pack with a lunch and a water bottle, compared to her full load. As she stepped aside to let me pass, I was surprised to see the beautifully aged face of a woman in her early seventies. She wore a chiffon scarf around her head, tied beneath her chin as my grandmother would have worn it. Wrinkles told the stories of past adventures, and the lines deepened as her face broke into a smile.

Twelve years ago, when my partner JoAnn and I hiked the Appalachian Trail, we were teasingly asked by other thru-hikers if we had brought our Geritol along. We were twenty-three years old, but, at that time we were two of the oldest thru-hikers on the trail. Back then, the most popular time to take off for a hiking journey was between college graduation and work. Things are changing. The American Hiking Society's figures show that more senior citizens are hiking than ever before. They have the time and money, and they recognize the obvious health benefits. The Appalachian Trail

Conference confirms these findings. And, as hostel keepers on the AT in Pennsylvania, we too have noticed that more and more senior citizens are taking on the physically and psychologically demanding sport of long-distance hiking. They put their dream on hold until the kids are grown and leave the nest, or until they can retire. They wait out their time for many decades, hoping their no-longer-young bodies can withstand the rigors of climbing up and down mountains while carrying heavy backpacks for months at a time. When the moment finally comes, the actual day of retirement, a few head off for the trail the very next day.

Mary Lee, who hiked the entire AT at the age of sixty-three, said, "Right at this moment, I feel as if I have to get out and do everything that I was going to do 'someday.' Someday is here."

I conducted a survey of some twenty-five senior hikers and discovered that most of them are crediting their performance to the way in which they've lived their lives. All of them have stayed consistently active through the years, have kept busy, and have been "participants" in life, not "spectators."

Sixty-seven-year-old Roland Mueser—an AT 2,000 miler—said, "My grandparents believed in exercise and the importance of spending some part of every day outdoors. Long before I knew this was 'healthy,' I exercised outdoors in many ways simply because it made me feel good."

Middle-aged people are realizing that hiking makes them feel good, too. More and more of them are taking a time-out from their stressful lives to hike. Many are dissatisfied and disillusioned with today's rat race and are taking to the trail to find answers.

Hiking has always been a wellspring for peace. John Muir knew it 150 years ago when he wrote, "Climb the mountains and get their good tidings. Nature's peace will flow into you as sunshine flows into trees. The winds will blow their own freshness into you, and the storms their energy, while cares will drop off like autumn leaves." In our hectic age, that advice is more priceless than ever.

Hikers, unfortunately, cannot be totally isolated from the ills of society nor from the demons that haunt some souls. "A hiker must be more realistic these days," says Brian King, public affairs director for the Appalachian Trail Conference (ATC). "The trail is not a fantasy land."

A few well-publicized incidents have alerted hikers to the potential danger of crimes along trails. Although many would like to think of trails as Edenic retreats from the ills of society, incidents of harassment, assault, and even murder are all occuring with greater frequency.

Members of the hiking community are fighting back. For example, the Conference and ATC-affiliated volunteers have spent hundreds of thousands of hours reconstructing and relocating hundreds of miles of the AT, both to improve its scenic quality and to improve security by removing the trail from roadways where most incidents involving harassment occur. They're repairing and moving dozens of shelters that are subject to vandalism, closing roads that provide too-easy access for the beer-party crowds, and preparing detailed computer-based records of reported incidents. ATC is also developing formal

Crime on the Trail

1. Do not hike alone. Hiking with at least one partner reduces the potential for harassment. It also provides security in case of accident or illness.

2. Inform others. Always leave your trip itinerary with family and friends.

3. Avoid provocation. Don't respond to taunts or attempts at intimidation.

4. Be friendly but cautious in your conversations with strangers you meet on the trail. Avoid people who act in a strange, provocative, hostile, or drunk manner.

5. Don't broadcast your itinerary to suspicious strangers, and avoid describing the whereabouts of your fellow hikers. If alone, claim to be part of, and ahead of, a larger group.

6. Camp away from roads and motor vehicles. Harassment is most likely in areas accessible to cars, including four-wheel-drive trucks. If concerned because of an encounter earlier in the day, hide your camp.

7. Carrying firearms is strongly discouraged. They are illegal in most areas if carried without a license or if concealed, and the odds are good that an innocent person may be hurt.

8. Eliminate opportunities for theft. Don't leave your pack unattended. If you must leave it, hide it carefully. Don't leave cash, cameras, or expensive equipment in cars parked at remote trailheads.

9. If you are the witness to or victim of harassment, promptly report the crime to local law-enforcement authorities (dial 911 or ask the operator to connect you to the closest state-police office) and also to the hiking organization or club responsible for the section, so that steps can be taken to enforce laws and prevent recurrences.

10. Never underestimate the importance of trail registers. Sign entries with your real name as well as any trail name you may be using, and report any suspicious activity there too. If trail volunteers need to locate you, or if a serious crime has been committed and authorities need more information, the first places they turn to are the trail registers. These registers are a powerful tool and can be essential to safety.

agreements with many state and federal agencies that are intended, in part, to encourage greater cooperation between law enforcement groups and other forms of emergency management. And through their various publications as well as responses to hundreds of thousands of written and telephone inquiries, they're advising prospective trail visitors to exercise reasonable precautions to avoid or minimize exposure to criminals.

The risk of an encounter is incredibly small, especially when viewed in light of the deaths caused by natural occurrences in the woods: lightning, exposure, and so on. Statistics-wise, the time spent behind a wheel, reaching the trailhead, is much more perilous than any amount of hiking on the trail. From 1974 to 1990 there were seven homicides on the Appalachian Trail. A few isolated incidents should not set off any major alarms.

Still, the human population in regions along many of our nation's trails is growing and will continue to do so. Trails are bound to become ever more crowded, and with this crowding will come an increase in the likelihood of unpleasant encounters.

Carrying a gun is not an alternative, and is highly discouraged. Unless you're using a gun for hunting, it does not belong on the trail. Not only is carrying a gun illegal in many instances, but also the chances of needing one are infinitesimal. The potential danger to other hikers of getting shot accidently by a novice who has been spooked by a night alone surrounded by owls, croaking frogs, and snorting deer, is too great to be chanced. Once a gun has been fired, you can't get the bullet back.

A few million hikers take to the Appalachian Trail

each year and most of them frequent portions that pass through high visitation areas such as the Shenandoah National Park, the Blue Ridge Parkway, the Great Smoky Mountains, the White Mountain National Forest, and certain state parks and forests.

Because of the crowded conditions on these sections of the AT, an extensive program of ridge runners and shelter caretakers is being employed in some areas. These individuals spend their days hiking sections of the trail, doing light maintenance work, and making sure it is open and clear. They can sometimes investigate specific management issues for local land-managers. Most importantly, though, they educate hikers on proper backcountry ethics and low-impact techniques.

The AT can get crowded on sections that pass in close proximity to major cities. There are areas on the Pacific Crest Trail in the Sierra Nevada, and in national parks known for their extraordinary beauty, that experience high trail traffic, too. If you're searching for a more solitary experience, you have to hike a popular trail in the off-season, or choose one of the lesser known and less frequently traveled trails that crisscross the country. That may sound easy, but 60 percent of all Americans walk for exercise or pleasure. Walking for pleasure is the most popular activity in the United States today, so it may take a little homework and traveling time to arrive at some of these lesser known trails for the experience you seek.

The United States has designated eight long-distance National Scenic Trails and nine National Historic Trails that could be a great natural resource, but unfortunately, the trails exist more on paper in filing cabinets than on

the ground. The plans have been drawn up, many since 1968, but the funds have not been allocated to make them a reality.

There are about 114,000 miles of existing trails in our nation's national forests. That sounds like a lot, but, according to a recent General Accounting Office audit of the U.S. Forest Service, 59,000 of those miles—more than half—are in need of work. These trails are plagued with health and safety hazards and otherwise fail to meet agency standards. Because of poor maintenance, 5,000 of these miles are classified as unusable.

The Forest Service admits it needs $260 million to bring the current trails up to par. Funding has fluctuated over the past decade and has been consistently less than what has been needed to keep the trails in good condition.

Consider, too, that we are sharing those miles with 40 million other hikers, and, according to the 1990 USFS Study for the Resource Planning Act, the demand for recreational trails will continue to grow rapidly in the future. Of the 22 outdoor recreational activities the USFS surveyed, day hiking and backpacking were projected to experience the most growth. Day hiking is expected to grow by 193 percent and backcountry hiking by 155 percent in the coming decades. In the 1980s alone, trail activities increased by 32 percent, even though trail budgets were cut.

Another growing concern is the alarming rate in which the lands that are designated as future trail corridors are being eaten up by developers, particularly in the East. This makes groups like the American Hiking Society— the only national nonprofit organization dedicated to

improving all of America's foot trails on public and private lands—very nervous. There is a growing concern that there won't be enough trails to accommodate the growing number of hikers in the future.

What to do? Write to your public officials. You do have a voice in the way our government spends its money and the way it thinks about the out-of-doors. Support an organization like the American Hiking Society, which is part of the National Trails Coalition, whose mission is to research the major problems leading to trail deterioration, to act on those findings through direct political action, and to provide financial support for trail advocacy groups. The coalition is not a membership organization, but by joining any of the groups involved in the fight for trails, you'll be supporting their activities.

Another marvelous way to ensure that trails will be here in the future is to be a volunteer. The 2,100-mile National Scenic Appalachian Trail was conceived and built and is now maintained almost entirely by volunteers. This kind of grass roots support is spreading all over the country, as millions of volunteers are building new trails and maintaining existing ones, often in partnership with federal and state agencies. The U.S. Forest Service, the Park Service, and the Bureau of Land Management are responsible for 90 percent of the nation's trails, most of which are found in the West. Construction and maintenance are usually contracted out to professional trail builders, but because of the backlog in trail maintenance, the fate of the trails cannot be left solely in the hands of federal agencies. The Appalachian Trail, with its strong

volunteer base and minimal governmental supervision, must be the model for the future; the burden of trail survival rests with us, the trail users.

The big question that is always asked is, why do trail volunteers sacrifice the comforts of home to scrape and strain on a trail? The work is often very hard. I remember how my relatively strong back rebelled after slamming a pick into the earth for hours. But I knew the experience was benefiting much more than my body, and I continued on.

Robert Freis, an AT end-to-ender and first-time volunteer trail worker, found the same thing to be true. "After several strokes I began to realize the immensity of building and maintaining the Appalachian Trail. Until then I had the narrow-minded views of an overburdened hiker, trudging along toward shelter, griping about roots or rocks on the trail without a clue as to the difficulty of clearing a 2,100-mile footpath. An hour after I began, I had wrought five feet of trail—maybe. Walking this trail is nothing compared to building it."

It's what happens to them after their work is complete that drives trail volunteers to keep swinging their picks. Seeing that footpath begin to grow and wind out of sight, when before there was no trail, is very gratifying. As Freis says, "Every shovelful of dirt is a link in the chain that binds all of us who love the trail, what it stands for, what it has done for us, and what it will do for future generations. They'll need it even more as their world becomes more crowded and complicated."

The bond between trail builders and hikers is one of time and distance and a shared vision. No matter where I

hike, when I see a stretch of trail that looks especially difficult to climb, I hurt a little less thinking of the builders' sweat and struggles. I know and appreciate what they've done so I might walk with greater ease. Many small jobs add up to amazing accomplishments and help make our nation's trails the asset that they are.

Unfortunately, despite the growing numbers of trail volunteers, according to the U.S. Forest Service's own research, they are not being used to their full potential in the national forests. Volunteers maintained more than 17,000 miles of trails in the national forests were maintained by volunteers last year, but 70 percent of all trail managers had to turn down volunteers because they lacked the personnel to plan trail work and supervise trail crews. Volunteer programs in the national forests, while potentially providing significant savings, do require funding and staff support and cannot be utilized to their full potential during times of inadequate budgets.

A more grass roots way of volunteering may be with the many individual trail clubs and organizations that are undertaking the monumental job of creating new trails, as well as maintaining existing ones.

Another, more personal way of ensuring that trails are here tomorrow is to practice low-impact techniques. As the number of trail users increases, so must our awareness of how our actions affect the environment. We can no longer affect a pioneer style of wilderness living. We are responsible for preserving the wilderness.

Most low-impact techniques are for ensuring that we as hikers leave the environment as we found it. With the increase in backcountry use, however, this is no longer enough. We also must be keenly aware of how we affect others who share the backcountry with us.

While mountain biking on the Chesapeake & Ohio Canal Towpath in Maryland, we stopped at one of the designated hiker-biker campsites for the night. Fishermen had illegally moved into the site for the three-day weekend, bringing a canoe full of luxuries from home. They took over the community picnic table with their coolers and supplies, forcing us onto the ground. Around 10 P.M. they pulled out their bright Coleman gas lantern and suddenly the night had turned to day. The inside of our tent shone a bright cerulean blue that kept us awake.

After a half hour, I got up and asked them if they could possibly light their candle lantern instead. Although they agreed, it was clear they didn't get the message, for they spent the next hour banging metal pots and pans as they did their dishes, pumping the noisy water pump to wash up, and slamming the spring-loaded outhouse door repeatedly. Another half hour passed before they finished their chores, and then they just moved a few yards away with their Coleman lantern and proceeded to sit around on lawn chairs, chatting late into the night.

The following night at another campsite, some campers began breaking up pieces of wood for a campfire, just as we were hitting the sack. They had been drinking beer all evening and throwing the bottles into the trash can with force so they would shatter and make a loud noise. I approached one of them and politely asked if they planned on being up late. He said yes and

they were also planning on setting off firecrackers. He thought "your children would enjoy them." I said our "children" is a baby—an eight-month-old baby—and she'd probably be very frightened. This man was considerate enough and/or sober enough to convince his buddies to move the firewood and the unlit campfire away, so that we might get some sleep. His friends were not as understanding, for they loudly broke more bottles and uttered profanities as they did so.

Many people go out into the backcountry with the idea that they're breaking loose from a regimented lifestyle and have every right to raise a little hell. Particularly if they're consuming alcohol, they have little or no idea of how they're behaving or how they sound. Let's hope that as the ideas of low-impact camping take hold, such people will increasingly realize that it is important to reduce our impact on each other, too. The whole idea of hiking and camping is to become one with nature and wilderness, and to appreciate the importance of all living things—including ourselves.

RESOURCES

How To Become A Volunteer

If you've got the itch to lay down some trail, you'll not want for opportunities. Some hiking clubs have operated trail crews for many years. The American Hiking Society's directory of volunteer positions in American parks and forests (see the list below) is another good resource.

You can work just about anywhere you'd like—close to home or far away. Bear in mind that transportation to base camp is usually your responsibility; if you're looking for a project in the Virgin Islands or Alaska, say, it could be costly. Once at base camp, however, most of your expenses are usually covered: lodging, food, transportation to and from the work project, tools and safety equipment, some group camping gear, and often a small weekly stipend for laundry and incidentals.

After picking a few positions that interest you, write or call the contacts listed and ask about aspects of the project that may not be contained in the brief catalog listing. You'll need to know what to expect in terms of weather, accommodations, benefits (if any), work difficulty, and responsibilities.

Despite the discomforts of aching muscles, blisters, wet clothes, insect bites, poison ivy, and lack of privacy, you'll be rewarded by the excitement of working in some of the most beautiful areas of the country, as well as the camaraderie and the satisfaction of learning and performing high-quality trail work. For more information about trail volunteer programs:

Adirondack Mountain Club, Volunteer Trails Program; Attn: Willie Janeway, Box 867, Lake Placid, NY 12946; tel.: 518/523-3441.

American Hiking Society, Volunteer Vacations Program, P.O. Box 20160, Washington, DC 20041-2160; tel.: 703/385-3252.

Appalachian Mountain Club, Reuben Rajala, Trails Supervisor, Box 298-A, Gorham, NH 03581; tel.: 603/466-2721.

Appalachian Trail Conference, Trail Crew Coordinator, P.O. Box 807, Harper's Ferry, WV 25425; tel.: 304/535-6331.

Earthwatch, 680 Mount Auburn St., P.O. Box 403, Watertown, MA 02272; tel.: 617/926-8200.

National Park Service, Office of Information, Attn: Volunteers in Parks Program, P.O. Box 37127, Washington, DC 20013-7127; tel.: 202/343-4747.

Sierra Club, Outings Department Service Trips, 730 Polk St., San Francisco, CA 94109; tel.: 415/776-2211.

Student Conservation Association, P.O. Box 550, Charleston, NH 03603; tel.: 603/826-5206.

You can also find volunteer positions as campground hosts, wilderness rangers, and backcountry guards. Wildlife surveys often require assistance, as do projects in biological research, photography, archaeology, and land surveys. You might want to horsepack supplies to rangers, man fire towers, write news releases, or serve on a cross-country ski patrol. If you want to gain experience, volunteering can open doors.

Request a copy of the American Hiking Society's publication "Helping Out in the Outdoors," which lists volunteer work opportunities in detail (American Hiking Society, P.O. Box 20160, Washington, DC 20041-2160; tel.: 703/385-3252; $5). □

Winter Solstice

Winter solstice. The day when the earth stops its southward journey through the sky and begins to move north again. From now on, days will grow longer and nights will shorten. Although winter begins today, the solstice promises new life: budding plants, returning birds, warmth. To the Lenni-Lenape Indians, who once lived in this area of Pennsylvania, the solstice was a time of great celebration.

My companions and I celebrate this event with a moonlit walk. Our destination is the Pinnacle, a promontory along the "endless" Kittatinny Ridge, sacred to the long-gone Lenni-Lenapes and an endangered area along the Appalachian Trail.

We step into the night. Clouds race across the moon's shining face, whose light is so bright you could read a book by it. Lights from nearby farms and homes along the road compete for our attention. So do the colored Christmas bulbs, blinking off and on. Not another soul is out on this special December 21st night.

Our wooded road soon enters the Pine Swamp, a misty, wet bottomland crammed with hemlocks and rhododendron, and steeped in folklore. The Indians were cruelly pushed out, but their spirit survived their destruction.

Moon shadows are still and sharp, like patches of sunlight and shade. Wind brushes the treetops; we hear its voice rush down the mountain, pass overhead, and move on in to the valley. When we break out into a high field, we can see we've gained elevation. More houselights appear, and fields in varying degrees of light and dark.

As we begin to climb over the Pinnacle, the treadway becomes so steep we have to dig the tips of our boots in sideways and walk gingerly, lest we slide backward. Branches wave and crack into each other across the face of the moon, for the wind is constant up here. My heart pounds, like the rhythmic drumbeat in the Lenni-Lenape rituals.

Soon the trail disappears in a steep boulder field, under the deep, dark shadows of a hemlock grove. We pick our way, using our hands as much as our feet, keeping our heads close to the ground. We grip the rough Tuscarora sandstone and scramble onto the summit and immediately feel the temperature drop.

The lights grab our attention first. Below us, they're scattered. Then tighter as our eyes travel up, we see the lights of the suburbs. At the horizon the sky is a bright, glowing streak. In the city, light-loving people are changing their night to day.

"They're encircling us," one of my friends says.

"Not to our sides," I answer. To our left and right the dark hulking Appalachian ridge stretched out like the backbone of a huge, sleeping creature. Darkness means wild, undeveloped lands. To us, that darkness means joy.

This land behind us needs to be preserved, I think. So do these farms below. We need wild places not only for pure water, clean air, and a place to rejuvenate our souls, but also because all things have a right to continue living as they have for millions of years.

We shiver. Time to head down. Sliding over the boulders, we use our rear ends and the backs of our legs as much as our hands and feet. The air warms and the wind slows as we descend.

As we enter the valley floor and see the crosses of light on the barn tops and the full solstice moon overhead, hope returns to our hearts. To the Lenni-Lenape Indians, the Great Spirit gave hope. To Christians it takes the form of a little baby.

But the form really doesn't matter—we're all connected to one another, and to all living things on earth. On our special moonlit walk on this winter solstice night, this belief has been reaffirmed. □

Low-Impact Techniques

• Avoid backpacking on holidays and weekends whenever possible. You'll not only help the environment, you'll avoid the crowds. Numbers also decrease dramatically in the fall and spring.

• Look for paths less traveled. Check with ranger stations for low-use areas. Consider hiking in Bureau of Land Management (BLM) areas and National Wildlife Refuge Areas. Trails near metropolitan areas or popular parks will have a higher percentage of day hikers. When backpacking in popular areas, plan a longer first day so that it is long enough to get you beyond the day hikers and into the more remote backcountry.

• Travel and camp in small family-sized groups. Camping areas are not designed for crowds. Large groups are often forced to spread out into untrampled vegetation, thereby destroying more land. Six should be your upper limit. If this isn't possible, divide your party into two groups and spend the night in separate camps.

• Take a litter bag to carry out all refuse, yours and others. All food garbage should also be packed out—every orange peel and eggshell. No one wants to see these while they're biodegrading. You shouldn't use the rationale that the animals will eat it—in most cases, it simply isn't true. Don't bury bones, extra food, or anything else. They'll be dug up by animals, who will leave the place a mess. Dispose of every cigarette butt, twistie, and pop top in your litter bag. Small, bits of seemingly insignificant trash have a way of multiplying and becoming a terrible eyesore. Before leaving an area, pick everything up. Burn your litter in a small trash fire if regulations allow, excluding foil and plastic, or pack it out in your litter bag.

• Carry a stove and choose foods that require little cooking. Don't use fires to cook on. In heavily used areas, most burnable wood is already used up.

• Never cut switchbacks, for they're built on steep slopes to prevent erosion. Walk single file in the center of the trail. When there's mud or water on the trailbed, don't cut around it or your footsteps will widen the trail and erode more land. Walk through the middle, where you envision the trail to be. The mud on your boots will dry in time. Travel cross-country only on rocky or timbered areas.

• Avoid "living off the land." Picking berries

or mushrooms is permissible even in most national parks, but know what you're eating and leave some behind. Otherwise, never pick or collect.

• Seek ridgetop or timbered campsites. Always avoid delicate, easily damaged shorelines by lakes and streams and fragile meadows. Instead, choose well-drained or rocky or sandy campsites. Make camp 200 feet away from lakes and streams.

• Never cut standing trees. If you must have a very small toe-warming campfire, and if conditions and the area you're traveling in allow it, use only downed and dead wood. Gather small firewood from timbered areas outside camp. If there is little or no wood available, that is an indication that the area is overused and all fires should be avoided. Make only small campfires in safe areas. They're appropriate only in already existing fire rings and in places where firewood is abundant.

• Avoid digging holes or trenches. Don't try to mold, change, adjust, manipulate, or carve the landscape. Don't uproot shrubs or plants to widen your site, nor cut pine boughs for a cushion under your sleeping bag. When clearing a site for your tent, don't slide your boot back and forth across the earth, thereby removing everything from the forest floor. Get down on all fours and lift pine cones, sticks, and stones with your hands, and keep the leaves and pine needles in place.

• Use lightweight boots if possible. Heavy, deep-lugged sole boots do much to contribute to excessive trail damage. They should be worn only for rough territory.

• Wash at least 100 feet away from water sources. Never clean pots and pans, feet, or anything else in the water source, but dip out water from your pot, walk away to do your washing, and deposit the dirty, soapy water away from the water source. Always use biodegradable soap, but never put it directly in the water source. Instead, use it in your pot of water, away from the area.

• Bury human waste four to six inches deep. Walk at least 200 feet away from all campsites, water sources, and drainage areas, and dig a small hole using a stick, stone, or backpacking shovel. After depositing your waste in the hole, cover it with the topsoil you removed. Tap down with your boot and place a rock or a branch on top of it. Never put anything but feces into the hole. Pack your toilet paper out in a Ziploc plastic bag or burn it when and where it's appropriate. Tampons, sanitary napkins, and disposable diapers should be disposed of in the same way. □

Jargon

Access trail—a trail that generally connects the main trail with a valley, roads, or other trail systems. It provides a critical link to towns so that long-distance hikers can resupply.

AYCE—all you can eat.

Bald mountain—a mountain with an open, grassy summit, void of trees, usually formed initially by grazing and often followed by forest management.

Basin—a bowl-shaped depression in the surface of the earth, often carved by glaciers.

Blazes—the generic term for trail markings, such markings include paint blazes, signs, cairns for treeless areas, and hatchet wounds on trees. Also, the specific term for painted marks on trees. The AT is marked with 2" x 6" white blazes placed at eye level going both north and south.

Bleeder—an angled depression built into the trail to drain water sideways off the treadway.

BLM—Bureau of Land Management.

Blowdown—large, uprooted, or broken trees that have fallen across the trail.

Blue-blazer—an AT hiker who walks a blue-blazed side trail instead of the official white-blazed route.

Body con—the use of food that your body craves, usually a high energy source, to convince it to perform and get you up the mountain.

Box canyon—a canyon that does not have a mouth, *per se*, or a sloping way out, but is surrounded on all sides by walls.

Break-in—a period of time that the body, the mind, or a piece of equipment takes to adjust and grow accustomed to exercise and the life of backpacking.

Breathable garment—an article of clothing coated with a certain substance that has microscopic holes that allows body heat (sweat) to escape. In waterproof breathable garments, the holes are not large enough to let rainwater through.

Buffer zone—the protective land area on each side of the treadway that insulates the hiker from activities such as home development, mining, or logging.

Butte—a hill rising abruptly above the surrounding area, with sloping sides and a flat top.

Cache—a hidden stock of supplies, especially food, hidden near the trail for future use.

Cagoule—a long, pullover raincoat that goes below your knees.

Cairn—a mound of stones constructed to mark trails in treeless areas. They are built to look artificial, are high enough to rise above the vegetation, and are often close enough to be visible through fog.

Camp robbers—any bird that frequents camp and picnic areas and is skilled at stealing unprotected human food. (Often jays, crows, ravens, nutcrackers.)

Causeway—an elevated treadway above saturated terrain filled in with rock, gravel, or earth, which provides a permanently hard and dry trail.

Chaparral—a dense thicket of shrubs and small trees, especially in the southwestern United States and Mexico, which can survive low annual rainfall and a rapid runoff of water.

Cirque—a steep basin, often containing a lake, and often located at the upper end of a mountain valley.

Clearcut—a logging practice whereby all trees are cut from the land (including saplings), not only select, mature trees.

Col—a pass between two peaks or a gap in a ridge.

Contour—when the trail is said to "follow a contour," it remains at equal elevation as it goes from one point to the next.

Counterbalance—a sometimes successful method of hanging food in a tree, to prevent animals from "scoring." Two food sacks of equal weight balance each other and eliminate the need to "tie off" a rope to a tree trunk.

Cranking—walking at a very fast pace; synonymous with being "in high gear."

Cross-country hiking—hiking across open country rather than following a trail.

Double blaze—two paint blazes on a tree, one two inches directly above the other, that are used to denote a change in direction or a junction on the trail.

Eminent domain—the right of a government to appropriate private property for public use, usually with compensation to the owner. Land for public trails is sometimes secured this way as a last resort.

End-to-ender—a backpacker who is traveling from one end of a long-distance trail to the other.

Ephemeral creek—a creek that flows for only a very short distance.

Flip flopper—a thru-hiker who begins at one end of a trail, goes partway to his goal, then flips to the opposite end of the trail and hikes back toward the end he originally came from.

Formidable ford—a river/stream crossing that is difficult to negotiate and causes fear, dread, and alarm in the mind and heart of the hiker.

Freshet—a sudden overflow of a stream, usually caused by a heavy rain or thaw.

Full-service town—a town near the trail that provides all the necessary services a hiker would need: grocery, restaurant, post office, bus station, and so on.

Giardiasis—a severe infection of the lower intestine caused by ingesting an amoebic cyst *(Giardia lamblia),* found in contaminated water. Symptoms include stomach cramps, diarrhea, bloating, loss of appetite, and vomiting.

Grade—the degree of inclination of the trail.

Greenhorn—a new, inexperienced hiker.

Green Tunnel—affectionate name for the AT since most of its route is beneath a canopy of trees.

Gulch—a small shallow canyon with smoothly inclined slopes and steep sides.

Half-gallon club—a "club" for AT thru-hikers who successfully consumed an entire half gallon of ice cream in one sitting.

Hostel—a place where a hiker can take time off from hiking to sleep, shower, and so on. They are typically inexpensive with spartan facilities.

Intermittent stream—a stream whose flow is interrupted by inadequate rainfall.

Knob—a prominent, rounded hill or mountain.

Lava tube—a cave or tube inside a lava flow formed by the liquid interior of a lava stream continuing to flow after the top and sides have cooled and hardened. When the hot lava has drained out, it leaves behind a hollow tube. Native Americans believe Sasquatch lived in such a place.

Layover day—a day off from steady hiking to rest, play, do chores, or tend to needs.

Pass—a way through, especially a narrow gap between mountain peaks.

Peak Bagger—one whose goal is to reach the summit of certain mountains, often in a particular geological area.

Pink snow—an algae found in alpine snow that is actually green but coats itself with a pink gel for protection from intense solar radiation. If ingested, it acts as a laxative.

Power hiker—a hiker who continually covers long distances day after day, often beginning very early in the day and hiking late into the night.

Prescribed burn—fires set by the U.S. Forest Service or the National Park System to reduce accumulated downed wood and thereby reduce future fire hazard.

Priming—building up pressure inside the tank of a backpacking stove so the liquid fuel can be converted to a gas and escape.

Privy—a latrine or outhouse.

Puncheon—a log bridge that is constructed to prevent damage to fragile wet terrain and provide a dry treadway to hike on.

Purist—on the AT, a hiker who hikes only the official AT, never misses a blaze, and never chooses to walk an alternate route.

Ravine—a deep narrow cleft or gorge in the earth's surface, especially one worn by the flow of water.

Re-entry—the physical and psychological process a long-distance hiker goes through when he leaves the familiarity of the trail environment and enters back into society and his former life.

Relo—a new stretch of trail that was built to replace a preexisting trail.

Rock flour—glacially ground rock that is reduced to fine, silty sediment, often causing creeks and mountain tarns to appear milky or greenish in color.

Runoff—rainfall that is not absorbed by the soil.

Saddle—a ridge between two peaks.

Scree slope—a slope with an angle of about thirty to forty degrees, consisting of small rocks and gravel that frequently collect under cliffs.

Seasonal creek—a creek that flows only during the rainy season.

Section hiker—a hiker whose goal is to complete a long-distance trail by hiking it in sections over a period of time.

Self-arrest—to stop yourself from sliding down a snow/ice slope by plunging or scraping your ice axe into the surface.

Sidehill construction—a trail built on the side of a steep slope that allows it to cross rather than climb straight up the slope, thereby minimizing soil loss.

Side trail—usually a dead-end trail providing access to features near the main trail, which allows hikers to visit interesting points that the main trail misses.

Skirt—to pass around a mountain, often at an even grade rather than to climb over it.

Slackpacker—a backpacker hiking a long trail who chooses to hike without his backpack and has other people shuttle the pack for him.

Slickrock—another name for southwestern sandstone that can be made slick to walk on by the loosened particles of sand that rub off when contact is made.

Slot canyon—a narrow canyon carved into sandstone by eons of rain and flash floods.

Snowbound—when a section of trail or an area of the mountains is buried under heavy snow and is virtually impassable.

Snowbridge—a bridge of snow, often over a creek, that is hollow underneath and could be very dangerous to walk over.

Spur ridge—a side ridge that emanates from the main ridge.

Stile—a structure that's built so hikers can cross

over a fence along the trail, without letting livestock out.

Sun cups—depressions in alpine snow initially beginning as little irregularities on the snow's surface, formed by rain and debris, and increasing to a depth of three feet by evaporation and heat absorption.

Switchback—a zigzagging sidehill trail of moderate to gentle grade used to climb a steep slope, thereby reducing erosion.

Talus slope—a slope with an angle of 45 degrees or greater where the rocks are larger and with sharper edges than those found on scree slops, resulting in greater friction and increased danger and difficulty in climbing.

Tarn—a small mountain lake.

Tent platform—a wooden platform used for staking tents at a campsite in order to control erosion of fragile alpine soils or reduce impact on a heavily used area.

Thru-hiker—a backpacker who is attempting to cover an entire long distance trail in one, continuous hike.

Toxic socks—a thru-hiker's socks after a few weeks of use on the trail.

Trail corridor—the treadway, the right of way, and all lands that make up the environment of the trail as viewed by the hiker.

Trailhead—the start of a trail, usually at a roadside.

Trail magic—term used to describe the wonderful, unexpected, and uncanny things that tend to happen to long-distance hikers on an extended journey.

Trail town—a town that a long trail goes right through or near enough, where hikers can resupply and attend to their needs, and whose citizens are usually sensitive to hikers and fond of them.

Trail widening—when a trail erodes and gullies to the point where hikers choose to walk on either side or detour around, resulting in trampled vegetation, a widened gully and multiple treadways.

Traverse—to go up, down, or across a slope at an angle.

Treadway—the trail bed where you walk.

Tunnel vision—what you experience when your trail topo map is so narrow that it gives you little indication of the land beyond the sides of the trail.

Two-thousand-miler—a hiker who has completed the entire length of the Appalachian Trail, either as a thru-hiker or a section hiker.

Undeveloped campsite—a campsite lacking in luxuries such as flush toilets, showers, hook-ups, and so on. *Maybe,* it will have a trash can and a picnic table.

Undulating trail—a trail that moves in a wavelike motion, often going in and out of numerous gullies.

Viewshed —all the land that comprises a view.

Wash—the removal or erosion of soil, subsoil, or the like by the action of moving water.

Waterbar—a rock or log barrier that diverts water off the treadway.

Watershed divide—a ridge of high land dividing two areas that are drained by different river systems.

Whiteout—a condition caused by a heavy cloud cover over the snow in which the light coming from above is approximately equal to the light reflected from below. In a whiteout there are no shadows, no visible horizon, and only very dark objects can be seen.

Yellow-blazing—when a long-distance thru-hiker hikes on roads for a section instead of on the officially blazed trail.

Yogi-ing —when thru-hikers behave/converse in a way that strangers who are picnicking or out for a short trip offer their excess food to them.

Yo-Yo-ing—the act of completing one long-distance thru-hike and turning around in the opposite direction to hike that same trail again (and again!). □

Popular Equipment Manufacturers

Asolo, Kenko International
8141 West I-70, Frontage Road North,
Aravada, CO 80002
tel.: 303-425-1200 (Boots)

Camp Trails/Eureka!
Box EB-385
Binghamton, NY 13902
tel.: 800/848-3673 (Tents)

Caribou Mountaineering, Inc.
46 Loren Ave.
Chico, CA 95928
tel.: 800/824-4143 (Tents)

Coleman/Peak I Products
P.O. Box 2931-AA
Wichita, KS 67202
tel.: 316/261-3211 (Stoves, sleeping bags, packs)

Danner Shoe Mfg. Co.
12722 N.E. Airport Way
P.O. Box 30418
Portland, OR 97230
tel.: 503/251-1100 (Boots)

Fabiano Shoe Co. Inc
850 Summer St. South
Boston, MA 02127
tel.: 617/268-5625 (Boots)

General Ecology
151 Sheree Boulevard
Lionville, PA 19353
tel.: 215/363-7900 (First Need water purifiers)

Gregory Mountain Products
100 Calle Cortez
Temecula, CA 92590
tel.: 714/676-6777 or 800/477-3420
(Internal frame packs)

Hi-Tec
4801 Stoddard Rd.
Modesto, CA 95356
tel.: 800/521-1698 (Lightweight boots)

Jansport
10971 72nd Place West
Painfield Industrial Park
Bldg. 306
Everett, WA 98204
tel.: 800/552-6776 (Backpacks)

Kelty Pack Inc.
1224 Fern Ridge Parkway
Creve Coeur, MO 63141
tel.: 800/423-2320 (packs)

Limmer Boots
Intervale, NH 03845
tel.: 603/356-5378 (Custom-made leather boots)

L.L. Bean
Casco St.
Freeport, ME 04033
tel.: 800/341-4341 (Sleeping bags, packs)

Lowe
P.O. Box 1449
Broomfield, CO 80038
tel.: 303/465-3706 (Packs)

Marmot Mountain International
2321 Circadian Way
Santa Rosa, CA 95407
tel.: 707/544-4590 (Sleeping bags)

Merrell
P.O. Box 4249
South Burlington, VT 05406
tel.: 802/869-3348 (Boots)

Moss Tentworks
Mount Bassie Street
Box 309
Camden, ME 04843
tel.: 207/236-8368 (Tents)

Mountain Equipment, Inc.
4776 E. Jensen
Fresno, CA 93725
tel.: 209/486-8211 (Packs)

Mountain Safety Research (MSR)
P.O. Box 24547
Seattle, WA 98124
tel.: 206/624-8573 (Stoves)

Mountainsmith
Heritage Square Building "P"
Golden, CO 80401
tel.: 800/426-4075 (Internal frame packs, tents)

Nike
1 Bowerman Drive
Beaverton, OR 97005
tel.: 800/344-6453
(Lightweight boots, rain gear, outdoor wear)

Northface
999 Harrison
Berkeley, CA 94710
tel.: 415/526-3530 or 800/654-1753
(Packs, tents, sleeping bags, outdoor wear)

Optimus
2151 Las Palmas Dr
Carlsbad, CA 92009
tel.: 800/543-9124 (Stoves)

Patagonia
Box 8900
Bozeman, MT 59715
tel.: 800/523-9597 (Outdoor wear)

Peak One/Coleman OutdoorProducts
250 N. St.Francis
P.O. Box 2931
Wichita, KS 67201
tel.: 800/835-3278 (Stoves)

Raichle Molitor USA, Inc.
Geneva Rd.
Brewster, NY 10509
tel.: 914/279-5121 (Boots)

Recreational Equipment Inc. (REI)
P.O. Box 88125
Seattle, WA 98138-2125
tel.: 800/426-4840 (Packs and boots)

Sierra Designs
2039 Fourth St.
Berkeley, CA 94710
tel.: 510/843-2010 (Tents, rain gear)

Slumberjack
P.O. Box 7048-A
St. Louis, MO 63177
tel.: 314/576-8000 (Sleeping Bags)

Technics
19 Technology Drive
West Lebanon, NH 03784
tel.: 800/258-7897 (Boots)

Therm-a-Rest
Dept. B
4000 First Ave.
South, Seattle, WA 98134
tel.: 206/383-0583 (Sleeping pads)

Timberland Co
11 Merrill Industrial Drive
Hampton, NH 03842
tel.: 603/926-1600 (Boots)

Tough Traveler
1012 State St.
Schenectady, NY 12307
tel.: 800/468-6844 (Child carriers)

Vasque, Division of Red Wing Shoe Company
314 Main St.
Riverfront Center
Red Wing, MN 55066
tel.: 612/388-8211 (Boots)

Walrus Inc
929 Camelia St.
Berkeley, CA 94710
tel.: 510/526-8961 (Tents)

Wilderness Experience
20721 Dearborn St.
Chatsworth, CA 91311
tel.: 818/341-5774 (Packs)

Zip Stoves 22 Corporation
10806 Kaylor St.
Los Alamitos, CA 90720
tel.: 310/598-3220 (Stoves) □

Food Suppliers

Alpine Aire
P.O. Box 926
Nevada City, CA 95959
tel.: 916/272-1971

Backpacker's Pantry, Inc.
1540 Charles Drive
Redding, CA 96003
tel.: 916/241-9280

Mountain House Oregon Freeze Dried
525 25th Ave. SW
P.O. Box 1048
Albany, OR 97321
tel.: 800/547-4060

Richmoor
P.O. Box 8092
Van Nuys, CA 91409
tel.: 818/787-2510

Stow-A-Way Industries
P.O. Box 957
East Greenwich, RI 02818
tel.: 401/885-6899

Trailwise
P.O. Box 8524
Green Valley Lake, CA 92341
tel.: 714/867-4992

Wee-Pak
P.O. Box 562
Sun Valley, ID 83353-0562
tel.: 800/722-2710

Mail Order Source Hiking Books

Backcountry Bookstore
P.O. Box 191
Snohomish, WA 98290
tel.: 206/568-8722

The Wilderness Bookshelf
5128 Colorado Ave.
Sheffield Village, OH 44054
tel.: 216/943-4143 □

Hiking Books

The Appalachian Trail Backpacker's Planning Guide, Victoria and Frank Logue, Birmingham, AL, Menasha Ridge Press, 1991.

Backpacker's Sourcebook, Noelle Liebrenz, Berkeley, CA, Wilderness Press, 1987.

Backpacking Basics, Thomas Winnett, Berkeley, CA, Wilderness Press, 1988.

Backpacking One Step at a Time, Harvey Manning, New York, Vintage Press, 1986.

Backpacking with Babies and Small Children, Goldie Silverman, Berkeley, CA, Wilderness Press, 1988.

The Boy Scout Handbook-10th Edition, Robert Birkby, Irving, TX, Boy Scouts of America, 1990.

The Complete Walker III, Colin Fletcher, New York, Alfred A. Knopf, 1987.

The Essential Guide to Hiking in the United States, Charles Cook, New York, Michael Kesend Publishing, Ltd., 1991.

Harsh Weather Camping, Sam Curtis, Birmingham, AL, Menasha Ridge Press, 1988.

How to Shit In the Woods, Kathleen Meyer, Berkeley, CA, Ten Speed Press, 1989.

Maps and Compass: A User's Handbook, Percy W. Blandford, Blue Ridge Summit, PA, TAB Books, 1991.

Mountaineering Medicine, Dr. Fred T. Darvill, Jr., Berkeley, CA, Wilderness Press, 1989.

Starting Small In the Wilderness, Marlyn Doan, San Francisco, CA, Sierra Club Books, 1976.

Winterwise, John M. Dunn, M.D., Lake George, NY, The Adirondack Mountain Club, 1988.

A Woman's Journey on the Appalachian Trail, Cindy Ross, Seattle, WA, The Mountaineers Books, 1987. □

Suppliers of Hiking/Backpacking
Equipment Catalogs

Campmor
P.O. Box 997
Paramus, NJ 07653-0998
tel.: 800/526-4784

Don Gleason's Camper Supply, Inc.
411 Pearl St.
Northampton, MA 01061
tel.: 413/584-4895

L.L. Bean
3651 Main St.
Freeport, ME 04033-0001
tel.: 800/221-4221
(request Sporting Specialities catalog).

Recreational Equipment Inc.(REI)
P.O. Box 88125
Seattle, WA 98138-0125
tel.: 800/426-4840 □

Magazines with Hiking Information

American Hiker, P.O. Box 20160, Washington, DC 20041-2160, tel.: 703/385-3252

Appalachian Trailways News, P.O. Box 807, Harper's Ferry, WV 25425 tel.: 304/535-6331

Backpacker, 33 East Minor St., Emmaus, PA 18098, tel.: 215/967-5171

Outside, 1165 North Clark St., Chicago, IL 60610, tel.: 312/951-0990 □

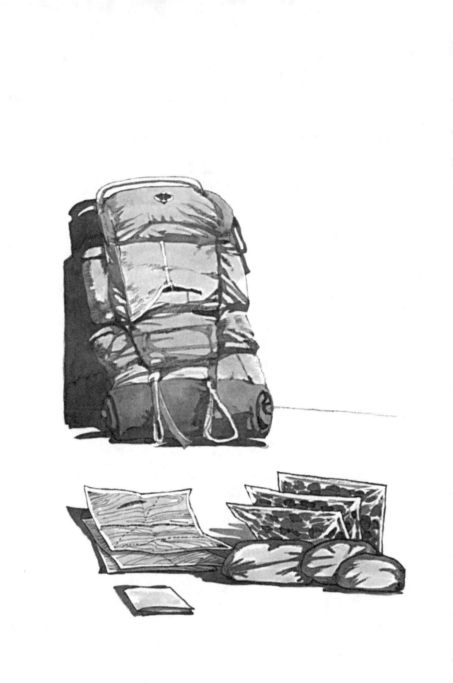

25 GREAT HIKES OF THE WORLD

By John Harlin, editor of Summit *magazine and author of*
The Climber's Guide to North America.

A self-styled Lord of the Trails—that's what
experienced hikers might think of anyone arrogant
enough to compile a short list of classic hikes of the
world. So let me hasten to explain my admittedly
subjective criteria. These two dozen or so walking
journeys are a selection from the hikes that keep my
appetite keen—whether I've gone on the hike or
simply dream of the day I can go.

It's a personal list: I didn't go prowling through
guidebooks (of which I have walls full) to unearth
something I'd never heard of. My first criterion was
that I had to know about the hike. Each of these hikes
has achieved enough of a reputation that, even if I
haven't done it, I'm very familiar with it and have
been hungry to do it for years.

For quite a few years now I've written guidebooks
and edited magazines about the outdoors, and my
mood continues to swing between wild enthusiasm
and depressing frustration. Enthusiasm for several
things: to reminisce over great places I've been,
to travel vicariously with others to the finest spots
on the globe, and to dream of the many new
places I keep discovering on paper. But then I
get frustrated: My dream list grows far more
rapidly than my ability to get to these wonders.

So I haven't included my complete, and lengthy,
dream list here. For the sake of the diverse tastes of

the many readers of this book, I've aimed for some balance in geography and hiking style. Beyond that, my biases include: (1) I like a hike with a goal. You'll find a number of destinations such as summits, oceans, and viewpoints; (2) I like to have something to look at, such as a view of mountains or oceans or canyons—or all three when I can get them; (3) I don't like to backtrack, so you'll find several hikes where you'll either have to arrange for transportation at the other end or travel in a loop; (4) I like to experience uniqueness in an area—to have a European experience be different from what's found in America, to have the West contrast as much as possible with the East (and vice versa); (5) I like to be entertained along the way by interesting walking—such as hiking on coral reefs or variable terrain; (6) I like to dream big (as in a super-long trail that takes months to hike) even though reality forces me to sample morsels of the whole instead.

So there you have it. If I've left your favorite hike out of my selection, just remember that when I wrote *The Climber's Guide to North America,* I included some 1,500 "classic" routes. It's frustrating to have such a long dream list. Be thankful that this list, at least, can be accomplished in a single lifetime of dedicated recreational hiking.

Major Tour Organizers

If any of these hikes whets your appetite, take a look under "Resources" for further information, suggested reading, and trip organizers. To get you started, I list only one outfitter for each trip, but you may want to check out some of the others listed below. Keep in mind that none of the hikes here requires a trip organizer; all you need are a dream, strong legs, a plan, and a desire to experience some of the world's most beautiful places.

Above the Clouds Trekking, Box 398E, Worcester, MA 01612, tel.: 800/233-4680.

Adventure Center, 1311-E 63rd St., Ste. 200, Emeryville, CA 94608, tel.: 415/654-1879 or 800/227-8747.

American Alpine Institute, 12122 4th M-28, Bellingham, WA 98225, tel.: 206/671-1505.

Himalayan Travel, Box 481-O, Greenwich, CT 06836, tel.: 800/225-2380.

Journeys, Dept. E, 4011 Jackson Rd., Ann Arbor, MI 48103, tel.: 800/255-8735.

Mountain Travel, 6420 Fairmount Ave., El Cerrito, CA 94530, tel.: 510/527-8100 or 800/227-2384.

REI Adventures, Box 88126, Seattle, WA 98138, tel.: 800/622-2236.

Sierra Club Outings, 730 Polk St., San Francisco, CA 94109, tel.: 415/923-5630.

Wilderness Travel, 801-OW Allston Way, Berkeley, CA 94710, tel.: 800/368-2794.

NORTH AMERICA

Eastern United States
Haystack Mountain, New York

Northeasterners often point out that bigger is not necessarily better—that the less awesome mountains on the eastern seaboard can be at least as beautiful as their more vertiginous western counterparts. Haystack Mountain is a magnificent example.

In the heart of the High Peaks region of New York's Adirondack Mountains, Haystack's rocky summit looks up at the boreal upper slopes of neighboring Mt. Marcy (5,543 feet), the highest point in New York. Separating the two peaks is the remote, trail-less Panther Gorge, in which steep, wooded slopes are a rich green through the summer and flecked with orange and yellow in early fall. Eastward, the view sweeps across the so-called Great Range, where one peak after another rises out of the dense forest, some peaks with 1,000-foot granite slabs on their flanks. All these high peaks are less than 5,000 feet high, and only the top slopes occasionally break the timberline. Stunning and vast though the view from Haystack is, it still leaves the impression of intimacy characteristic of Eastern mountains.

Allow two days for the 20-mile round-trip hike from Adirondack Loj. Late summer and fall are best, but if you're willing to use skis or snowshoes, you can make the trip in the winter.

Resources

Information and trip organizer: Adirondack Mountain Club, 174 R.R. 3, Box 3055, Lake George, NY 12845, tel.: 518/668-4447.

Reading: Guide to Adirondack Trails: High Peaks Region, *by Tony Goodwin (Glens Falls, NY: The Adirondack Mountain Club).*

Hump Mountain, North Carolina and Tennessee

The Southern Appalachians are a sea of gently rolling hills. Like a rogue wave, an occasional high mountain, sometimes a series of them connected in a long, flowing ridge, pierces the tranquil surface. From these vantages, you can put into perspective the densely forested "hollers"—where seeing the forest can literally be impossible for all the trees.

Roan Mountain, at 6,286 feet, is the highest point in the region, but neighboring Hump Mountain is more open and provides perhaps the most expansive views in the southeast. Because this is the eastern seaboard, your eyes can't avoid a few distant encroachments of civilization. Yet the scene becomes increasingly wild as you focus on the foreground, with its hundreds of acres of open meadow, its incredible flowering shrubs (in sequence: dogwood, mountain laurel, azalea, rose-purple rhododendron, white rhododendron), and the velvety softness of form that seems to flow from your feet to the most distant of hills. There, the hazy horizon finally merges forest and sky.

Allow two days to hike the 20 miles round-trip, or

add more days to take a longer loop hike. The hike can be made at any time of year, although spring and fall are preferable.

Resources

Information: Tocane Ranger District, U.S. Forest Service, Box 128, Burnsville, NC 28714, tel.: 704/682-6146.

Reading: Tennessee Trails, *by Evan Means (Chester, CT: Globe, Pequot Press).*

The Long Trail, Vermont

Yes, it is long—265 miles—and it doesn't exactly get you from point A (Vermont's Massachusetts border) to point Z (Vermont's Canada border) with a great deal of efficiency. But the whole notion behind hiking the Long Trail is enjoying points B through Y, not necessarily getting from one end of the trail to the other.

One of the oldest long-distance recreational hikes in North America, the Long Trail was established during the early decades of this century. The builders must have foreseen the Great Depression, for this trail is designed to lift your spirits along with your body. Wherever possible, it finds a ridge to follow: Where the trees open enough for a view over the rolling Green Mountains, there you'll find the Long Trail. It seems to skirt every pond in Vermont, and the terrain in the northern reaches is rugged as well as beautiful.

Allow a month to hike the entire trail, or do it in sections of any length. You can hike most of the trail early spring through late fall.

Resources

Information: Green Mountain Club, Inc., Box 889, Montpelier, VT 05602, tel.: 802/223-3463.

Trip organizer: Country Inns Along the Trail, R.R. 3, Box 3115, Brandon, VT 05733, tel.: 802/247-3300.

Reading: Guidebook to the Long Trail, edited by Brian Fitzgerald, (Montpelier, VT: Green Mountain Club).

U.S. MOUNTAIN STATES

Longs Peak, Colorado

This is the only one day "hike" I'm recommending that takes you to a summit above 14,000 feet. In the official rating system used in mountaineering, this hike is categorized as a Class 3, meaning you'll need to use your hands, but not a rope, to help you along in the rough spots. You'll need a good set of lungs, too, as the hike starts at around 9,000 feet and continues —7 miles later—to the 14,255-foot summit. Is it worth it? Several thousand people a year seem to think so. On the way up the Keyhole Route (the easiest route up the mountain) you'll pass views of the spectacular east face of Longs, with its 2,000-foot vertical plunge. (As an acclimatization hike, take the 5-mile walk to 12,000-foot-high Chasm Lake at the base of the east face. This view is, in fact, more spectacular than anything you'll find on the summit hike itself.)

The "trail" to the summit winds almost completely around the mountain, taking in vistas up and down the spine of the Continental Divide, over to the forested western slope, and across the plains of eastern Colorado. What's more, you'll get a taste of the mountaineering experience without having to venture into the technical aspects of the sport. Although the Keyhole Route does not require climbing experience when it's in good condition, it can become quite tricky when conditions are not so good, so check with a ranger the day before you head up. This mountain is very real and sometimes very serious; it demands respect.

Allow a full day for the hike/climb. Many parties start at three or four in the morning and return in the early afternoon to avoid thunderstorms; the need to do this depends on prevailing weather patterns. The best season is July and August.

Resources

Information: Rocky Mountain National Park, Estes Park, *CO 80517, tel.: 303/586-2371.*

Reading: Rocky Mountain National Park: Classic Hikes and Climbs, *by Gerry Roach (Golden, CO: Fulcrum).*

Devil's Garden, Utah

Although most of the hikes in this selection involve days, even weeks or months, of perambulation, Devil's Garden in Arches National Park can be scampered through in a few hours. But what outrageous hours. A gentle trail explores 9 miles of the most tortured yet bizarrely beautiful landscape Dante could have invented. Fully 64 natural arches have been sculpted out of the desert's red sandstone, the longest being Landscape Arch, a 291-foot span that is stretched so thin in places that it's in danger of crumbling. But arches are just the brightest flames in this infernal landscape. My great joy here is discovering delicately balanced boulders, freakish towers, and contorted canyons. From high points, and sometimes through the arches themselves, you can catch glimpses of the snow-covered La Sal Mountains.

Devil's Garden can be experienced in a few hours, but allow more time if you can. Spring and fall are the best times to go, but the hiking can be done year-round.

Resources
Information: Arches National Park Headquarters, Box 907, Moab, UT 84532, tel.: 801/259-8161.

Trip organizer: Sierra Club Outings, 730 Polk St., San Francisco, CA 94109, tel.: 415/923-5630.

Reading: Hiking the Southwest's Canyon Country, *by Sandra Hinchman (Seattle, WA: The Mountaineers).*

Teton Crest, Wyoming

From the flatlands of Jackson Hole, the Teton Range shoots upward more than 7,000 vertical feet to a seemingly impenetrable tangle of summits (highest point: the Grand Teton summit, at 13,770 feet). Up close, however, valleys open and a passage through (in fact, a complete circuit around most Teton summits) reveals itself.

The Teton Crest trail can start with a 4,000-vertical-foot tram ride at the Jackson Hole ski area, followed by Granite Canyon's wide-open wildflower fields. Otherwise, hikers walk up past Death Canyon's towering granite walls. Either way, you soon reach a fantastic, 200-yard-wide shelf, with cliffs below and above. In a few miles, a gentle pass brings you to the wildflower displays of Alaska Basin, nearly garish in their enthusiastic bursts of color. One more pass and glacier-carved Cascade Canyon leads you gently through forest glades back down to Jackson Hole. This trail certainly provides you with some of the finest walking in the Rocky Mountains.

Allow two to four days to cover the distance: 33 miles from the tram or 30 miles from the Whitegrass parking area. The best time of year is summer—for the weather and the wildflowers.

Resources

Information: Grand Teton National Park, Drawer 170, Moose, WY 83012, tel.: 307/733-2880.

Trip Organizer: Jackson Hole Mountain Guides, Box 7477 T, Jackson, WY 83001, tel.: 307/733-4979.

Reading: Hiking the Teton Backcountry, *by Paul Lawrence (San Francisco, CA: Sierra Club Books).*

WESTERN UNITED STATES

Plateau Point, Arizona

The great chasm of the Grand Canyon not only carves into the staid desert landscape, it carves into the souls of those who come to see it as well. It's impossible not to be moved by the sight of this gash in the earth—a mile deep, 7,000 feet rim-to-rim, filled with a self-contained world of sandstone mountains, side canyons, and plateaus. Plateau Point perches on the brink of a cliff that plummets 1,200 feet to the raging waters of the Colorado River. Even here, you are already well inside the body of the canyon, with the north and south rims both 4,000 feet above.

Your eyes take in a panorama of "temples" (as many of the buttes are called), mesas, and massive walls. As the sun sets, the whole world turns orange, and you can fairly feel the canyon growing around you. Walking in and out of the canyon is often hot, dusty, and crowded, but there are very good reasons indeed that people come from around the world to take this hike.

Allow a full day to make a strenuous round trip (it's 6 miles one-way) on the Bright Angel Trail, or camp along the Colorado River and return the next day via the South Kaibab Trail (15 miles total). The hike can be made any time of year, although cold and snow in winter and blistering heat in summer are likely.

Resources

Information: Grand Canyon National Park, Box 129, Grand Canyon, AZ 86023, tel.: 602/638-7888.

Reading: Hiking the Grand Canyon, by John Annerino (San Francisco, CA: Sierra Club Books).

John Muir Trail, California

For slightly more than 200 miles, the John Muir Trail winds through some of the most inspiring high country in the United States. It's hard to know when to stop with the wonders of this land: sun that is almost always shining, open vistas that look across 13,000- and 14,000-foot peaks, meadows overflowing with wildflowers, literally thousands of alpine lakes, 5,000-foot-deep canyons —plenty of places to escape your fellow hikers.

If you start from the north in Yosemite Valley, you'll first wind through the mist of waterfalls and past sweeping granite faces in one of the most extraordinary sections of California. Then you break into the high country, where the trail maintains an elevation between 9,000 and 11,000 feet for most of the distance, then climb to the summit of 14,494-foot Mt. Whitney, highest point in the contiguous United States. Pause for a while to gaze westward over thousands of square miles of roadless wilderness, then hike the last 15 miles east to the pavement at Whitney Portal. If you can't do the whole thing, then sample either end for a few days.

Allow about two weeks for the complete hike. The

best time to go is during the summer—whenever the mountains decide summer should begin and end.

Resources

Information: Sequoia and Kings Canyon National Parks, Ash Mountain, Three Rivers, CA 93271, tel.: 209/565-3456.

Trip organizer: Sierra Club Outings, 730 Polk St., San Francisco, CA 94109, tel.: 415/923-5630.

Reading: Guide to the John Muir Trail, *by Thomas Winnett (Berkeley, CA: Wilderness Press).*

Olympic Beaches, Washington

Each tide that floods the Pacific shoreline of Olympic National Park washes new trophies ashore. When the waters withdraw, the beaches are covered in flotsam, and the tide pools team with life. Offshore, sea otters loaf and bald eagles swoop down to pick fish out of the water. But it's the sea stacks that I find unforgettable—100-foot-tall, weirdly sculpted towers of basalt, often with a single tree balanced on the summit, and speckled with the bright-red blooms of Indian paintbrush.

As you hike down the sandy beaches, you'll find your path blocked occasionally by rocky headlands that jut into the water. The rain forests that cover the headlands are lush with long green tendrils of sphagnum moss. You can pick from two stretches of coastline, one 16 miles and the other 22 miles long. The most popular is the stretch southward from La

Push, offering one to five days of hiking, depending on how far you want to go before doubling back. Fuel for campfires is never a problem, as driftwood is piled high on the beach.

Allow one to four days for either stretch, depending on how far your curiosity carries you. The hike can be made year-round, although summer is best.

Resources

Information: Olympic National Park, 600 E. Park Ave., Port Angeles, WA 98362, tel.: 206/452-4501.

Reading: 100 Hikes in the South Cascades and Olympics, *by Ira Spring and Harvey Manning, (Seattle, WA: Mountaineers Books).*

Wonderland, Washington

Had it not blown its top into the jet stream, Mt. Rainier would likely be the highest peak in the lower 48 states. It's certainly the most impressive, lifting its classic volcanic cone 14,410 feet above nearby Puget Sound. Unlike most mountains, Rainier rules alone, with no distracting satellite peaks. The 92-mile walk around its glacier-encrusted flanks yields views to all points of the compass: south to the smoldering remains of St. Helens, west to the Olympic Mountains and the waters of Puget Sound, north to the rugged North Cascades, and east to the logged clearcuts of Snoqualmie National Forest. But, always, the bulk of many-faceted Rainier towers nearly 10,000 feet above you.

The Wonderland Trail hugs the mountain, hovering at about the 5,000-foot level and leading through virgin forests, into the most phenomenal wildflower meadows in the northwest and past cascading streams milky white with sediment known as glacial flour. A bonus: It's an easy trail to do in pieces, even as a series of day hikes. Allow one to two days for sections and one to two weeks for the whole circumnavigation. The best time of year is early to late summer, depending on the mountain's unpredictable moods.

Resources

Information: Mt. Rainier National Park, Tahoma Woods, Star Rte., Ashford, WA 98304, tel.: 206/569-2211.

Trip organizer: REI Adventures, Box 88126, Seattle, WA 98138, tel.: 800/622-2236.

Reading: 50 Hikes in Mt. Rainier National Park, *by Ira Spring and Harvey Manning (Seattle, WA: Mountaineers Books).*

Lake Chamberlain, Alaska

The Arctic National Wildlife Refuge's Mt. Chamberlain, at 9,020 feet, is the highest point in the Brooks Range. To the south the range extends into barren, snow-specked mountains, where the tread of human feet is rare indeed. But to the north you can wander over the tundra as it sweeps gently out of the mountains and down the coastal plain to the Arctic Ocean.

Lake Chamberlain is simply a convenient landing place for a floatplane and a starting point for excursions that can last for days, weeks, or months in any direction. This is a magical place, where nearly 200,000 caribou come every year to calve, grizzly bears and wolves are expected sights, and birds overwhelm you with their numbers and diversity. I hesitate to bring more people to this, one of my favorite and one of the wildest places on earth. But the controversy surrounding oil drilling in this area—controversy that will go on year after year until the coastal plain gets official wilderness protection—demands that people know how special the place is to ensure that it won't be violated.

Allow as much time as you can afford. The hiking season runs from June through August.

Resources

Information: Alaska Public Lands Information Center, 250 Cushman St., Fairbanks, AK 99701, tel.: 907/451-7352.

Trip organizer: Arctic Treks, Box 73452, Fairbanks, AK 99707, tel.: 907/455-6502.

Reading: Adventuring in Alaska, *by Peggy Wayburn (San Francisco, CA: Sierra Club Books).*

Ruth Gorge, Alaska

The Ruth Amphitheater has been likened to a larger Yosemite Valley set in the Pleistocene Age. From the famous Mountain House—a cozy cabin built by the legendary glacier-pilot Don Sheldon for climbers and ski tourers—you look out over an unfathomable collection of granite walls up to 5,000 feet high. Ice pours off peaks in every direction, and snaking down the valley floor is the Ruth Glacier, a veritable frozen Amazon. When the clouds part, you'll see, towering above it all, Denali itself—The High One—otherwise known as Mt. McKinley, the highest peak in North America.

There's a catch here: You'll need skis to get around the Ruth Amphitheater, but I think of this trip as hiking on skis. The terrain is so level (unless you choose otherwise) that no skiing experience is necessary. Should you desire a one-way trip instead of a series of jaunts from the Mountain House, ask your ski-plane pilot to land as high up the glacier as he dares, and travel downhill until you reach your prearranged pickup point.

Allow a few days or a couple weeks, depending on how much territory you want to cover. The best time to go is April through June; May is ideal.

Resources
Information: Denali National Park, Box 9, Denali, AK 99755, tel.: 907/683-2294.

Trip organizer: Alaska-Denali Guiding, Inc., Box 566, Talkeetna, AK 99676, tel.: 907/733-2649.

Reading: The Best Ski Touring in America, *by Steve Barnett (San Francisco, CA: Sierra Club Books.)*

LONG TRAILS OF
THE UNITED STATES

The Appalachian Trail, the Continental Divide Trail, the Pacific Crest Trail

New long-distance trail systems continue to be developed, but there will always be the classic big three: the Appalachian Trail (AT), the Continental Divide Trail (CDT), and the Pacific Crest Trail (PCT). No, I admit that I haven't walked the length of any of them. I've nibbled here and chewed there, but I've only been able to dream of devouring the whole of each—2,100 miles, 2,700 miles, and 2,600 miles, respectively.

Each has its own personality. The AT travels through deciduous forest, sometimes breaking out for a view but more often reaching through a tunnel of trees. This hike tends to be a social journey because nearly 100 "thru-hikers" complete the trail each year, and many, many more commit themselves to shorter sections. The PCT, on the other hand, travels through a tremendous variety of terrain, from the desert near Mexico to the high passes of the Sierra and the rainy forests of the Cascades. Relatively few people attempt to hike this trail end-to-end in a given year. Finally, the CDT is so wild and rugged that few have ever made the complete hike. In fact, the exact location of the route is still under debate.

Among the hikes I've already mentioned, I've cited excerpts from these Long Trails—for example, the

John Muir Trail in California and Vermont's own official Long Trail. These are the standard way to taste the magnificent megatrails, but I couldn't make a list of the world's great hikes without giving full credit to the big three themselves.

Allow approximately six months for each trail (and if you have time to do an entire trail, I'm envious), depending on your speed. For the western trails, great care must be given to choosing starting times to avoid high-country snows.

Resources

Information: The Appalachian Mountain Club, 5 Joy St., Boston, MA 02108, tel.: 617/523-8636. Continental Divide Trail Society, Box 30002, Bethesda, MD 20824. Pacific Crest Trail Conference, 365 W. 29th Ave., Eugene, OR 97405, tel.: 503/686-1365.

Reading: Guide to the Appalachian Trail, *by Jim Chase (Harrisburg, PA: Stackpole Press);* Guide to the Continental Divide, *by James R. Wolf (Bethesda, MD: Continental Divide Trail Society);* The Pacific Crest Trail, Volumes 1 and 2, *by Jeffrey Schaffer (Berkeley, CA: Wilderness Press).*

CANADA

Berg Lake, British Columbia

Chances are you won't even get a glimpse of Mt. Robson, the peak you're here to see, so often is it veiled in clouds. And as you wait for a view you'll hear and probably feel in your bones the crashing sounds of glacier ice calving into the lake.

But if and when the storm clouds clear, the mountain shines brilliant in sheets of ice and crumbling walls of semifrozen shale. Mt. Robson has long been regarded as the monarch of the Canadian Rockies, and from its massive flanks broken glaciers plunge dramatically into Berg Lake, milky white with glacial flour. The walk to Berg Lake passes through mixed evergreen forests before reaching a stiff uphill grade along the Valley of the Thousand Falls. If you want to extend your trip by several days, continue on to link up with the North Boundary Trail in Jasper Park.

Allow two days for the 28-mile round-trip hike. The time to go is spring through fall; snow is likely by early October, and bad weather possible any time of year.

Resources

Information and trip organizer: Alpine Club of Canada, Box 1026, Banff, AB TOL OMO, tel.: 403/762-4481.

Reading: The Canadian Rockies Trail Guide, *by Byron Patton and Bart Robinson (Banff, AB: Summerthought Press).*

ASIA

Annapurna Circuit, Nepal

Welcome to the heart of the Himalayas—a continuous, 24,000-foot plunge from ice-encrusted summits to the bottom of a subtropical gorge—the deepest valley in the world. The 200-mile circuit around 26,545-foot Annapurna (the first 8,000-meter peak to be climbed) crosses a dizzying array of climates and landscapes. But, considering the ruggedness of the terrain, the trail is amazingly comfortable to walk. That makes sense: The route has stood the test of time, being part of the ancient trading path connecting isolated Buddhist villages and faraway coastal cities.

From the highest pass, 17,770-foot Thorong La, your eyes can wander forever across the seemingly barren Tibetan plateau. Keep in mind that this is not country to rush around in. Allow three to four weeks for the circuit in order to acclimatize properly. The hiking can be done year-round; although, to avoid monsoon season, early summer is best.

Resources

Information: Embassy of Nepal, 2131 Leroy Pl., Washington, DC 20008, tel.: 202/667-4550.

Trip Organizer: Himalayan Travel, Box 481-O, Greenwich, CT 06836, tel.: 800/225-2380.

Reading: Trekking in Nepal, West Tibet, and Bhutan, *by Hugh Swift (San Francisco, CA: Sierra Club Books);* Fodor's Himalayas.

EUROPE

The Irish Sea to the North Sea, England

What could provide a more enticing invitation to long-distance walking than a hike across England from the Irish

Sea to the North Sea? Here you can travel for two weeks along heather- and moor-covered ridges and past ancient stone monuments, pausing for pub grub one day and a picnic on a wild escarpment the next and sleeping in bed-and-breakfasts along the way.

Beginning in the world-famous Lake District, Britain's favorite mountain-holiday destination, this journey takes in the best of a landscape of rugged but rounded hills. It then continues east through the dales of Yorkshire and the moors of North York. Industrialized towns and highway crossings are blemishes on the natural landscape, but my dominant memory is one of wilderness, pastoral countryside, and charming English villages. Most of the route is easy to follow, but you can wander off the track in places. Fortunately, variants are often just as delightful.

Allow about two weeks for the 190-mile walk. It's possible to hike this route year-round, but, for the best weather, go from April to November.

Resources

Information and trip organizer: Sierra Club Outings, 730 Polk St., San Francisco, CA 94109, tel.: 415/923-5630.

Reading: Classic Walks in Great Britain, *by Bill Birkett (Newbury Park, CA: Haynes Publications).*

FRANCE/ITALY/SWITZERLAND

Tour du Mont Blanc

Medieval goatherds knew that the Alpine peaks were inhabited by dragons. The roar of rocks cascading down unseen couloirs, the clap of thunder, and the fiery dance of lightning in cloud-covered summits kept all but the most intrepid away. Now, however, the Alps sing siren songs to mountaineers the world over, and the village of Chamonix, at the foot of 15,782-foot Mont Blanc (highest peak in the Alps), has become the mountaineering center of the world. There's no need to dangle from granite walls to experience these mountains: The Tour du Mont Blanc carries awed hikers around the peaks in a 100-mile loop. A network of huts provides full dinners and rooms, but you'll probably prefer the privacy of your own tent.

Allow seven to 12 days for the entire hike, which can also be done in pieces. You can camp, stay in huts and hotels, or plan a combination of all three.

Resources

Information: French Government Tourist Office, 610 5th Ave., New York, NY 10020, tel.: 900/990-0040.

Trip Organizer: Mountain Travel, 6420 Fairmount Ave., El Cerrito,CA 94530, tel.: 510/527-8100 or 800/227-2384.

Reading: 100 Hikes in the Alps, by Ira Spring and Harvey Edwards (Seattle, WA: The Mountaineers).

The North Sea to the Mediterranean; the Netherlands, Belgium, Luxembourg, Switzerland, and France

If you can't decide what walk to take in Europe, why not roll them all into one and do a megawalk of Europe from top to bottom. In French, the trail is called the Grande Randonné Cinq, or GR5 for short, and it's semiclearly marked along its entire 1,500-mile length.

No, you won't find many people walking the route from end to end. As with the American long trails, the vast majority of hikers pick portions to cover on any given vacation, hoping to link them over a period of years. Unlike the American long trails, however, this is no self-contained wilderness walk. You could carry a tent, I suppose, but it may be a lot easier to grab a hotel room at the end of a day, whether you're walking through the open fields of Belgium or the forests of Luxembourg, over French mountain passes or down Mediterranean hillsides. You could carry a stove and cook some lunch, but it would be easier to stop in a bistro for a sandwich and café au lait.

Allow as much time as you can afford and do as big a chunk of the trail as you can—about 3½ months for the whole thing. You can travel anywhere in summer; most places, except the higher Alpine passes, are accessible during the rest of the year.

Resources

Information and trip Organizer: Mountain Travel, 6420 Fairmount Ave., El Cerrito, CA 94530, tel.: 510/527-8100 or 800/227-2384. (Note: Mountain Travel does not offer this specific trip but can provide route information and arrange a customized trip upon request.)

Reading: Walking Europe Top to Bottom, *by Susanna Margolis and Ginger Harmon (San Francisco, CA: Sierra Club Books).*

Kleine Scheidegg-Lauterbrunnen or Zermatt-Gornergrat, Switzerland

Sure, these are different hikes with different mountain views, but the spirit of each is so similar that I just can't bring myself to choose between them. Each offers you a unique Alpine hiking experience foreign to most Americans—a trip up a lift (in these two cases, by cog railway) and a leisurely but spectacular walk back down. Of course you could hike up as well.

If you start the first hike at Kleine Scheidegg (above Grindelwald), you'll pass beneath that famous triumvirate of peaks—the Eiger, Monch, and Jungfrau. If you start at the Gornergrat, you'll be regaled with exquisite views of the Matterhorn and Monte Rosa. Either way, you'll be awed by Switzerland's most famous mountains as you wander through a pastoral Alpine setting complete with cow bells and the requisite chalets.

Allow several hours for each of these 7½-mile hikes. Late spring through early fall is the best time to go, unless you choose to don skis.

Resources

Information: Swiss National Tourist Office, 260 Stockton St., San Francisco, CA 94108, tel.: 415/362-2260.

*Reading:*100 Hikes in the Alps, *by Ira Spring and Harvey Edwards (Seattle, WA: The Mountaineers).*

SOUTH AMERICA

Inca Trail, Peru

There's no question that the 30 miles from Kilometer 88 (where the train drops you off) to Machu Picchu is where the world's trekkers come to walk in South America. Although its reputation for crowds and armed robbery dampened my enthusiasm for this hike, I encountered no such troubles, and the allure soon became clear: views of glaciated peaks from 14,000-foot passes, walks through subtropical cloud forests and giant orchids, descents to rugged canyon floors, camping in open meadows by cascading streams. But the highlights were the miles of cobblestoned Inca trails, including steps carved through a tunnel, and the four major Inca ruins, some in superb condition.

Allow three to four days for the one-way hike (return by train). Go May through October to avoid the rainy season. Porters and a guide may not be necessary for experienced, acclimatized hikers, but they certainly make the trip less of an ordeal, and they can be helpful in avoiding an encounter with bandits.

Resources
Information: Peruvian National Tourist Office, 800 Brickell Ave. No. 815, Miami, FL 33131, tel.: 305/374-1579.
Trip organizer: Journeys, 3516 NE 155th, Seattle, WA 98155, tel.: 206/365-0686.

Reading: Adventuring in the Andes, *by Charles Frazier (San Francisco, CA: Sierra Club Books.)*

SOUTH PACIFIC

Milford Track, New Zealand

Rarely does a place shine through the rain as does New Zealand; with scenery like this, soggy days seem to be washed out of memory. The Milford Track, most popular and best known of New Zealand's many tracks (trails), is a case in point. From the village of Te Anau, you motorboat for miles down a deep blue lake to the trailhead. From there, you trek some 33 miles through exquisite subtropical rain forests filled with the calls of exotic birds, over MacKinnon Pass with its phenomenal views of snowy peaks, and down to the deep waters of the Milford Sound (part of Fjordland National Park).

This is a rain forest, so be prepared for rain. Along the way, however, are two large wilderness huts and hotels at Te Anau and Milford Sound offer all the conveniences.

Allow three days to complete the 33-mile distance. December through March is the best time to go.

Resources

Information: New Zealand Tourist Office, Suite 530, 630 5th Ave., New York, NY 10111, tel.: 212/698-4680.

Trip organizer: Above the Clouds Trekking, Box 398E, Worcester, MA 01602, tel.: 800/233-4499.

Reading: Tramping in New Zealand, *by Jim DuFresne (Berkeley, CA: Lonely Planet Publications).*

FRENCH POLYNESIA

Tahiti-Iti, Tahiti

Tahiti? *Tahiti?* That's a typical reaction when I tell people that perhaps the most exotic, most fascinating hike I ever made was on this Polynesian tourist trap of an island. It turns out that the eastern end of Tahiti-Iti (Little Tahiti, the peninsula that protrudes from the island like a Siamese twin) is just too rugged to put roads and hotels on. Besides, this is where the legendary ghosts hang out. But there is a route that takes you from one road terminus to another.

You'll spend about a third of the time walking through the water on coral reefs, a third of the time on narrow beaches between the jungle and the sea, and a third of the time scrambling (and I mean crawling sometimes) up and over deep-jungle headlands, across cliffs that plunge into the surf, through natural tunnels in the rock, and dashing across wave-pounded bays. The hike is difficult even for the skilled, but it's a fantastic tropical experience.

Allow two to three days for the 25-mile hike, or a week to loop back through the interior. The hiking season is year-round, though July and August are the coolest and driest months.

Resources

Information and trip organizer: OPATTI (National Tourist Bureau), Fare Manihini, Boulevard Pomare, BP 65, Papeete, Tahiti.

Reading: Tahiti and French Polynesia: A Travel Survival Kit, by Robert F. Kay (Berkeley, CA: Lonely Planet Publications).